STEPCHILDREN OF MUSIC

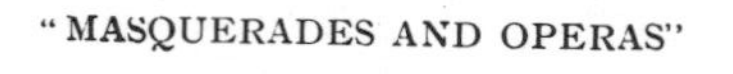

"MASQUERADES AND OPERAS"

ENGRAVING BY HOGARTH

STEPCHILDREN OF MUSIC

BY

ERIC BLOM

Essay Index Reprint Series

BOOKS FOR LIBRARIES PRESS, INC.
FREEPORT, NEW YORK

First published 1926
Reprinted 1967

LIBRARY OF CONGRESS CATALOG CARD NUMBER:
67-28731

PRINTED IN THE UNITED STATES OF AMERICA

CONTENTS

ILLUSTRATIONS

INTRODUCTION

INTRODUCTION

ALTHOUGH there seems at first sight to be no connection between the subjects discussed in this volume, their choice was not an entirely fortuitous one. The works dealt with are, it is true, chosen freely from two centuries of musical history, and they stand in no family relation to each other ; but they are linked together by the pathetic circumstance of having come into the world to be Music's stepchildren, ignored by the public at large, and scarcely likely to be made the subject of special study by the professional critic, who is busy with topical matters, or for other reasons deems it unprofitable to bestow his attention on music that would seem to him to belong, in Butler's words, " to a debatable class between the subreputable and the upper disreputable."

Even musicians who evince the greatest curiosity in the music of the future are seldom aware that their inquisitiveness might be equally well employed were they to investigate the forgotten or half-remembered music of the past, or at least to give personal attention to works of more recent date which have never been accepted, or are already dismissed, by the bulk of their colleagues. It is indeed a fascinating pastime to speculate on the ultimate position of a new composer, but it is no less amusing and stimulating to visit some vaguely-familiar musician of the past and consolidate an acquaintance with him which was previously based solely upon rumour. He will generally be found to be a personality very different from that pictured by the historian who contents himself with repeating the verdict of tradition. Sometimes we may find that he has been unduly extolled, but more often that he is scandalously slandered; in either case he will prove a discovery.

Some of the stepchildren of Music bear the name of an almost forgotten composer, with whom they share an obscurity they by no means deserve; others were fathered by great men, of whom they are so utterly unworthy that the master's admirer thinks it more expedient to ignore them altogether. It may seem as vulgar to pry into the sins of the great as it appears unprofitable to remember the virtues of the humble, but once we are led by sheer curiosity to examine such matters of relative unimportance, we begin to realize how immensely productive they are of new thoughts bearing on more vital things.

This collection of desultory essays may, it is hoped, give the reader a taste for exploring the byways of musical history. There is much that is interesting among Nature's freaks and stunted growths, and a withered tree here and there is not unattractive, if only by contrast, among many verdant ones. Why, then, should we pass by the rarities and anomalies in music? It seems incredible, for instance, that among the thousands who listen time and again to Tchaikovsky's fourth, fifth and sixth Symphonies, no matter whether with relish or aversion, scarcely anyone should ever evince a desire to know if the first three might not possibly please them as much, or better. It cannot be taken for granted that a composer always progresses upward, as may be gathered from a perusal of Mendelssohn's Piano Sonatas, if it may be permitted to go on quoting examples from the chapters of this volume. How entertaining, and frequently delightful, it is to know small composers by their works, and not merely by their names, the study of such minor figures as Galuppi, Lampe, Philidor or Lortzing proves convincingly; and a glance at characteristic products of a particular period, such as "The Dragon of Wantley" or "Le Devin du Village," however imperfect they may be as works of art pure and simple, illuminates for us whole pages of the musical history that revolves around them. Again, why should we be content to accept for ever the usual derogatory view of Piccinni, when it must be obvious to every thinking musician that only a personality of no small calibre could have been set up by a powerful and intellectual party as a serious rival to Gluck? What reason is there for considering the examination of Beethoven or Wagner at their worst as a profitless impertinence? How can the strength of César Franck be estimated with fairness, unless we know his peculiar weakness? Must we shut our eyes to a species of music in which Max Reger excels because we have made up our minds that he is an inferior composer?

Let us do justice to the minor artist, and allow him to please us, if he can; let us, likewise, be irreverent enough to divert ourselves by contemplating the indiscretions of the great. It is amusing to watch the youthful Rossini fumbling with a medium that does not suit him or Samuel Butler dabbling in one not properly his own; but it is also agreeable to see Liszt discarding all shallow mannerism when he sets out to give us of his best in a work which few care to know; it is instructive to follow Cherubini, Roussel, Delius, Strauss or Bartók into one particular field of their art in which they may or may not be at home, or to observe Arnold Bax unlocking the rusty padlocks of a gate leading into one that has long lain fallow; it is wholesome to witness the tragedy of explorers like Chabrier and Pedrell, who were broken, the one by misunderstanding, and the other by a strenuousness of labour that defeated its own ends; and it is useful to discover the causes of the rapid downfall of a Serov, or of the neglect of a work like Elgar's "Falstaff."

An acknowledgment is due to the Editor of

Musical Opinion for such portions of these essays as appeared in the pages of that journal. Once or twice the author has ventured to repeat more or less verbally a phrase previously used by him in the programmes of the New Queen's Hall Orchestra or in the columns of the *Manchester Guardian*. If such auto-plagiarism be considered reprehensible, his excuse must be that, having found no better way of giving new shape to an irrevocable thought already expressed through a more transitory medium, he thought it preferable to preserve it, for what it may be worth, in the original form.

But enough of apology, unless it be for the author's light treatment of his subjects, which could no doubt have been dealt with far more learnedly. Technicalities and historical information, however, were not the main object of these studies, although as much of the kind as seemed desirable for general utility has been included. The author's real aim was a form of criticism which could not be accused—whatever else its defects—of following the two main currents of present-day musical journalism, with neither of which he is much in sympathy. If this little volume can lay claim to any originality, it will perhaps be that of displeasing equally the two factions which reproach each other respectively with an exclusive worship of established reputations and with an excessive zeal in creating new ones; but if the book only convinces a few of its readers that the study of Music's stepchildren is not a wholly useless occupation, it will have achieved all it set out to do.

I. AN OFFSHOOT OF THE BEGGAR'S OPERA

I. AN OFFSHOOT OF THE BEGGAR'S OPERA

THE extraordinary success of the first English ballad opera stimulated a bevy of literary and musical coxcombs of the early eighteenth century to imitation. During the decade following 1728, the year of the production of "The Beggar's Opera," at least forty more or less entertaining satires and farces allied to old ballads and popular songs made their appearance with varying success. Subsequently the rage abated considerably, but it was not until thirty years after Gay's masterpiece that the species became extinct, destined to remain fruitless in its own country, but becoming the direct forebear of a foreign type of musical stage entertainment, the *Singspiel*, which was engendered through the popularity of Charles Coffey's "The Devil to Pay," and its sequel, "The Merry Cobbler," in Germany.

To fit ready-made tunes to a book of often deplorable nonsense and doggerel was a characteristic occupation of an age in which many authors would willingly sacrifice their artistic conscience to so facile a method of acquiring lucre.

> These handy Hirelings can, in half a Day,
> Steal a new Ballad Farce from some old Play:
> To mangled Scraps of many an Ancient Tune
> Tagg Feetless Jingle, Jarring and Jejune.
> The jaded Play'rs with equal haste rehearse,
> 'Till Sing Song limps to Horrid! Hobbling Verse.

Thus wrote Henry Carey in an epistle addressed to the Earl of Chesterfield in 1735, when a ballad opera of his own* had been rejected by the management of Drury Lane Theatre. Carey, whose indignation was not unmixed with rancour, never attempted another work of this kind; but he is responsible for a piece which, although no legitimate offspring of "The Beggar's Opera" on the musical side, reveals its literary line of descent from Gay's work. The burlesque opera, "The Dragon of Wantley," so well known to the historian by name, yet frequently taken to be the musical as well as the literary production of the author and composer of "Sally in our Alley," is not a ballad opera, but a work newly composed. Excellent musician that he was, Carey would no doubt have found it easy, without recourse to a fellow artist, to garnish his verses with some favourite tunes, if not to invent new ones. In his discouragement, however, he took no part in the musical portion of the work, and entrusted its composition to John Frederick Lampe—or better, Johann Friedrich, for he was a German by birth—a musician all but forgotten to-day, but highly esteemed by his contemporaries, not excepting Handel.

To study "The Dragon of Wantley" is to experience a twofold surprise. From the vogue which the piece once enjoyed, we expect a

* "The Wonder; or, an Honest Yorkshireman."

I. Faber Fecit

Harry Carey

brilliant, biting satire, or at least an amusing intrigue; but what we discover is a fairly good imitation of the hopeless dullness of Italian opera plots of the period, and a none too amusing exaggeration of the *niaiserie* of their words. The book is mildly comic at best, not from its wit so much as from a deliberate exclusion of wit.

The second surprise is a more pleasant and startling one: Lampe's music is so good that one wonders how it can have been so utterly forgotten. It is a glaring illustration of the sad fact that the fame of composers of the past depends much more on the extent of their success and the circumstances of their activities than on the quality of their work. How anxious we should all be to know a newly discovered hundred and fifty-fourth symphony by Haydn, or whatever its number might be, were it to compare ever so unfavourably with those we already possess; but who takes the trouble to make the acquaintance of a delightful work by a man whose name does not happen to strike our imagination? To the musician of to-day Lampe is simply a supernumerary in the brilliant stage picture the chief figure of which is Handel, and no one thinks it worth while to enquire into his individuality.

Lampe's origin is obscure; all we know of his youth is that he was born about 1703, somewhere in Saxony. He came to London in 1725, began his career as a bassoon player at the opera, and some five years later was engaged by Rich to compose music for pantomimes and other pieces for Covent Garden. From this point his history becomes more precise. He came into contact with Carey before 1732, when he wrote music to the latter's opera, "Amelia." Hawkins tells us that Carey was his pupil, but little faith can be placed in this notoriously untrustworthy historian, and since Carey was considerably the elder of the two, and had learnt from Geminiani and Roseingrave, it seems more likely that the parts of master and pupil were reversed, if indeed they were ever enacted. "The Dragon of Wantley" was produced in 1737 and proved so great a success that the following year a sequel appeared under the title of "Margery, or a Worse Plague than the Dragon," which shared the common fate of such supplementary ventures. The association with Carey then ceased; in 1741 Lampe wrote the masque, "The Sham Conjurer," and, after the latter's death, the mock opera, "Pyramus and Thisbe," which appeared in 1745. Two theoretical works by Lampe, "A Thorough Bass Method" (1737) and "The Art of Musick" (1740) were highly esteemed, and twenty-four hymn tunes to words by the Rev. Charles Wesley became familiar. Lampe died, an honourable and honoured man, at Edinburgh on July 25th, 1751, and Wesley wrote a hymn on his death, which was set to music by Arnold.

His epitaph, too, reflected the sincere admiration of his contemporaries, but proved sadly unprophetic in saying that "his harmonious compositions shall outlive monumental registers and with melodious notes through future ages perpetuate his fame."

Whoever does not know Lampe's music may be pardoned for concluding, from the surroundings in which it originated and from the success it enjoyed, that it must be the work of one of the numerous imitators of Handel who led a parasitic existence at that time. How surprising and refreshing it is, therefore, to find that the music of "The Dragon of Wantley" has scarcely anything in common with Handel, but a great deal with Bach. It is small music, but it rewards one's curiosity richly enough, were it only because it throws light on the dim history of the composer's youth. For it seems, indeed, almost impossible to anyone who studies this score that Lampe should not have been a pupil of Bach. We know that he was born in Saxony, and it is easy to imagine that he may have been a pupil at the St. Thomas School in Leipzig when Bach became cantor there in 1723. The connection of these two musicians, if it ever existed, can only have lasted eighteen months, or at the most a couple of years, but Bach's great personality could easily impress itself on a receptive youth in so short a time. At any rate, the influence is proved beyond question by the music to "The Dragon of Wantley."

Carey shall be made to tell his unspeakably silly plot in his own words, found in the argument he solemnly prefixed to the opera book :

"Wantley in Yorkshire, and the adjacent Places, being infested by a huge and monstrous Dragon, the Inhabitants, with Margery Gubbins at their Head, apply to Moore of Moore-Hall, a Valiant Knight, for Relief; he falls violently in Love with Margery, and for her Sake undertakes the Task; at which Mauxalinda, a Cast-off Mistress of his, is so enraged that she attempts to kill Margery, but is prevented by Moore, who reconciles the contending Rivals, kills the Dragon, and has Margery for his Reward."

It will be seen that there is scarcely any resemblance to "The Beggar's Opera" in the main outlines,* but there are numerous details which clearly betray their paternity, more especially the scenes between Margery and Mauxalinda, nothing more or less than a coarsened imitation of those between Polly and Lucy. Clearly, the opera-goers of the period did not soon tire of allusions to the hand-to-hand fight on the open stage between Francesca Cuzzoni and Faustina Bordoni at a performance of Bononcini's "Astyanax" in 1727, which Dr. Arbuthnot

* The plot is, in fact, a parody of Handel's "Giustino," produced earlier in 1737.

and Colley Cibber exploited as well as Gay and Carey.

The quarrelling duet:

> Insulting Gipsey,
> You're surely tipsey,
> Or *non se ipse*,
> To chatter so.

may serve as a specimen, not only of Carey's shameless plagiarism, but at the same time of his wretched humour and miserable verse-mongering. The whole work is a shallow farce with scarcely any touch of genuine satire, and wherever the author makes an attempt at chastising some vice or folly, he is content with the pale reflection of a thought already expressed much more pointedly by Gay. Such things as the following are simply watered-down ideas from "The Beggar's Opera" and "Polly":

> O give me not up to the Law,
> I'd much rather beg upon Crutches;
> Once in a Solliciter's Paw,
> You never get out of his Clutches.

The trouble with Lampe is that he took the whole thing seriously. His music is far too good for this sorry stuff; it has a way of intensifying the inanities and at the same time ruining itself by the association. Who knows but that it would have been preserved for posterity, had it been allied to a libretto worth the saving. As music pure and simple it could be revived to-day without any adaptation. There is nothing cheap, nothing flimsy about it. It is shapely, profound, dramatic, and has a seriousness mingled with grace that seems to belong to a Bach rather more under French influence than John Sebastian himself ever was. A German musician living in England need not be reproached for having nothing southern about his art, but for a skit on Italian opera, his music, which has neither frivolity nor humour, certainly is totally unsuitable. All the characters, including the Dragon and the Knight, whom Carey compels to rant like naturalized British Fafners and Siegfrieds, sing their idiotic burlesque words with a fervent gravity fit for a Lutheran cantata. Even the final chorus is treated with genteel seriousness in spite of the absurd words :

> Sing, sing and rorio
> An Oratorio
> To gallant Morio
> Of Moore Hall.
>
> To Margereenia
> Of Roth'ram Greenia,
> Beauty's bright Queenia
> Bellow and bawl.

Margery commiserates with the Squire's children, whose breakfast has been devoured by the monster, in an air that is worthy of a Bach Passion: a lovely plaintive Sicilienne with beautiful vocal lines intersected by delicious little oboe phrases.* There is even the intensely sorrowful pause on the chord of the diminished seventh, so evocative of Bach. Mauxalinda's first song is no less dramatic and beautiful, and no more appropriate. It is difficult to point out particularly fine passages without detailing almost the whole score. There is good part-writing everywhere, interesting treatment of the basses, exquisite harmony with frequent use of chords of the diminished seventh and occasionally even of the major ninth, and splendid declamation often giving an unexpected rhythmic turn to the words. Conventional tricks, such as the sequence, are exceedingly rare. The vigorous drinking song of Moore, the love duet with the charming imitations between the voices, the quarrelling duet with its conflicting parts, the dramatic air of Margery while the fight is in progress, all this is as delightful as it is incongruous.

Who can tell whether the prediction of Lampe's epitaph would not have been fulfilled, had only his charming music been allied to a subject that appealed to his temperament? In any case, it is time for the musician to realize that the work, generally passed over by the historian as entirely

* The part of Margery was sung by Mrs. Arne's sister, Isabella Young, who became Lampe's wife.

Carey's, owes its only admirable feature to another composer but for whose unfortunate choice and consequent oblivion the world would be the richer by a comparatively unimportant but lovable little work.

As for Carey's share in this ballad opera, it is interesting to note that the idea of scoffing at the favourite device of introducing a dragon into the plot was no more his own than various other details of the piece. One of Hogarth's earliest plates, "Masquerades and Operas," published in 1724, bears the following inscription:

> O how refin'd how elegant we're grown!
> What noble Entertainments Charm the Town!
> Whether to hear the Dragon's roar we go,
> Or gaze surpriz'd on Fawks's matchless show,
> Or to the Opera's or to the Masques,
> To eat up Ortelans, and empty Flasques
> And rifle Pies from Shakespears clinging Page,
> Good Gods! how great's the gusto of the Age.

II. "BRAVE GALUPPI"

A SONATA BY GALUPPI FROM A CONTEMPORARY MS.

II. "BRAVE GALUPPI"

NEXT to Domenico Scarlatti, there is no finer eighteenth-century Italian harpsichord composer than Baldassare Galuppi (1706-1785). But Scarlatti himself, although one of the most original artists of all times, being still insufficiently appreciated, it is perhaps hardly surprising that the smaller Galuppi should be nothing more than a name to most musicians. It must be said that the fault lies chiefly with the publishers, who have been slow to devote their activities to the works of either of these two splendid figures of the Italian *settecento*. Only lately a complete edition of Scarlatti's sonatas has at last been published,* and still more recently has a selection of twelve sonatas by Galuppi, edited by Giacomo Benvenuti† been given to the world. Another collection of the latter is in the catalogue of the "National Edition of Italian Music"‡ that likewise contains a series of arias from one of Galuppi's operas,§ of which he wrote about a hundred, a fact that perhaps explains his small output for the harpsichord as compared with Scarlatti's five hundred Sonatas.** A thematic list published in the

* Ricordi & Cie, Milan.
† Pizzi & Cie, Bologna.
‡ Istituto Editoriale Italiano, Milan.
§ "Il Filosofo di Campagna."

** It is rather curious, and not a little suspicious, that the sonatas in the complete Scarlatti edition should number exactly five hundred.

" Rivista Musicale Italiana "* by F. Torrefranca gives twenty-eight as the number of Galuppi's Sonatas, but there is a remark to the effect that two edited by Pauer and one by Köhler are not included in the list. In establishing a comparison between the two composers it must be remembered that Scarlatti's sonatas are almost invariably detached movements, while in those of Galuppi two or three movements are gathered together, which brings their number to about eighty.

The Sonatas mentioned in the thematic list, the MSS. of which are scattered about the libraries of musical institutions at Brescia, Bologna and other Italian cities, appear to have remained unpublished, with the exception of the first six, described as " Opera Seconda," which were issued by Walsh in Catharine Street, Strand, probably in or about 1741, when Galuppi came to England as conductor to the King's Theatre, Haymarket, after the failure of Handel's management. The last six sonatas were composed at Venice in 1782 for the Grand Duke Paolo and the Grand Duchess Feodorovna.

Galuppi seems to have had no more than a fair success in England, where he, like his contemporaries, was eclipsed by what may have been the genius or merely the popularity of Handel. Burney comments on the " hasty, light and flimsy style " that then reigned in

* 1909; Vol. IV

Italy, which "Handel's solidity and science had taught the English to despise." But even Burney, like everyone else at the time (and indeed much later), was swayed by Handel's tyrannical genius that advanced, as it were, in massed formation and crushed everything that was less robust. Handel, who could afford to be rude, not only to kings and courtiers, but even to *prime donne* and tenors, wrote music calculated to elbow its way in front of that of others by the sheer weight of the said "solidity" (or should it read "stolidity"?). On the other hand, on looking through the arias from "Il Filosofo di Campagna"* one is almost inclined to agree with Burney. In these arias Galuppi's invention, though not devoid of a certain charm, utterly lacks individuality, and there is no evidence of even as little sense of character as we find in the operas of Mozart's boyhood. Yet it cannot be doubted that, although he wrote no opera of lasting value, he must have paved the way to many later reforms. He did something, for instance, to develop the *finale* which Mozart was destined to raise to its greatest glory, and there must have been some modern and daring touches about his music. Burney mentions him as the first to use "B flat as a passing note against

* The most successful of the operas, on a libretto by Goldoni, which was performed in London in 1761 and in Dublin, as "The Guardian Trick'd," in 1762.

B natural "* and, next to Porpora, "the sharp fifth in melody," an early glimpse of the augmented triad. And the same historian says: "Indeed, many of the refinements in modern melody and effects in dramatic music seem to originate from the genius of Galuppi, at least in England." Still, if a balance were to be drawn, little enough would probably remain to the credit of Galuppi in the domain of opera.

Not so with the harpsichord music. Galuppi's sonatas are unlike those by any other composer of his time. He introduced, above all, the sonata in several movements, at any rate to Italy. So far as he knew, he introduced it to the world, for it is extremely unlikely that he could have known and emulated the work of Philipp Emanuel Bach. The one-movement form had reached its highest development in Scarlatti, whom Galuppi was not content merely to imitate. But his emancipation did not go very far beyond form, and on beginning to play the Sonatas we are inevitably reminded of Scarlatti, a comparison that can only be unfavourable to the younger composer. Only a careful examination leads to the discovery of characteristic features that would be vainly sought in the more original, more daring, and more high-spirited Scarlatti. There is a certain breadth and dignity, an amplitude

* There is an analogous passage in the Allegro of the eighth sonata in the Benvenuti collection, p. 82, bar 9.

of phrase, lacking in the latter, and a greater variety of movement conducive to a more widely diversified range of emotion. Many of the Sonatas have an almost Mozartian tenderness which we never come across in the shrewd, mordant, waggish Scarlatti, who on the other hand, in his unromantic art, steers more safely clear of a sentimentality from which his younger rival is not altogether free. Galuppi, of course, can be charmingly witty at times, but his humour is always more sedate and decorous than Scarlatti's bouncing, swaggering raciness. Scarlatti cares less about convention, he is freer, more impudent, less obedient to the formalities of the period; in short, he is the more modern of the two. Galuppi occasionally annoys us by his use of stereotyped eighteenth-century patterns, which were resorted to by the composers of the time to prop up their more anæmic ideas. The worst of these artifices, the "Alberti bass," is absent in Scarlatti, for even when very occasionally passages resembling it occur in his sonatas, they invariably have some thematic or structural significance and are never used as mere padding. These *rococo* trappings bring Galuppi somewhere near Mozart, but he never seems able to transcend the formula completely, and even to endear it to us like a trait in a familiar face that we would be loth to miss, as Mozart at his best undoubtedly does.

Benvenuti's selection contains some fine examples and covers as wide a range of expression as may probably be found in the whole of Galuppi's harpsichord work. In the first movement of the tenth Sonata the editor has seen fit once or twice to suggest an *ossia* that will hide the clash of semitones between the melody and the accompaniment or a progression in fifths, an act of academic timidity that seems pardonable only because it draws one's attention to these little touches of early audacity. Even if it is argued that they may be the result of carelessness rather than of daring, they are sufficiently quaint to be worth retaining. The Sonatas contain many other features, like three-bar rhythms, suspensions, chromaticisms, that must have sounded very modern once. Suave and graceful as they are on the whole, several of the movements sometimes rise to grandeur. The first movement (*larghetto*) of the second Sonata is worth a Bach Prelude in the "48," while that of the twelfth (*andante spiritoso*) suggests the Matthew Passion. The *andante* of the third is very daring and dramatic. The first movement of the fifth foreshadows Mozart, and its deliciously crisp and much more individual *allegro assai* is one of the most charming movements in the whole collection. The seventh Sonata opens with a lovely *largo*, which is followed by an exhilarating, rather Handelian fugue, a fine piece of free counterpoint. There is less contrapuntal writing than in Scarlatti, with his very persistent imitative openings; Galuppi, although his music is always transparent, seems concerned less with strict part-writing than with a truly " pianistic " (if the term may be applied to harpsichord music) disposition of his material. Another very beautiful slow movement is that of the eleventh Sonata, which is set off by an *allegro* of Haydn-like vivacity. The form of nearly all the movements is somewhere between that of Scarlatti and the fully developed sonata form of Haydn and Mozart. There are usually two parts, the beginning of the second presaging the more modern working-out section by restating in a different key usually the first subject, occasionally the second subject, and sometimes a new subsidiary idea.

Compared with the Scarlatti Sonatas, those of Galuppi are relatively easy to perform. One has, in fact, to guard against the temptation of playing them too rapidly. While the former, with their rattling vivacity, can hardly be played fast enough save by a few exceptionally nimble pianists, the latter require a kind of lingering, caressing touch, if the bloom of their graceful tenderness is not to be brushed off. Unlike the more ostentatious Scarlatti, who always seems to play to an appreciative assembly, watching with delight the effect of his brilliant sallies, Galuppi sounds as if he were playing dreamily to himself, or at most to a few intimates grouped round him and listening in half-troubled, half-soothed silence, waiting for the end of the piece to utter words of praise resembling those imagined by Browning :

Brave Galuppi ! that was music ! good alike at grave and gay !
I can always leave off talking when I hear a master play.

III. THE PHILOSOPHER, THE ACTRESS, AND THE BOY

III. THE PHILOSOPHER, THE ACTRESS, AND THE BOY

ON October 18th, 1752, the court of Louis XV was astir at Fontainebleau. It witnessed the first performance of a little opera, or an *intermède*, as it was called : "Le Devin du Village." The occasion was a great one. The composer was no other than Jean-Jacques Rousseau, the famous Mademoiselle Fel sang the part of the heroine, the King and the Queen were present, and there was a brilliant gathering of their elegant and frivolous retinue. The great writer and philosopher was flattered into the belief that he was an equally great composer, and the piece was so successful that the performance had to be repeated six days later. It made an irresistible appeal, perhaps by way of reaction, to a society who had already been prepared by the author's writings to respond to his plea for a return to the simple things of nature, but who only succeeded in carrying their charming affectations and their varnished corruptions with them into the open air. The shepherds and shepherdesses, the pastoral plays, the rustic pictures of the period, all show a desire for nature frustrated by the mannerisms of a civilization too deeply steeped in artificiality to be cured by any less cruel awakening than a Revolution. Even Rousseau himself, though he preached the gospel of simplicity, did not altogether succeed in carrying out his ideals in his work. "Le Devin du Village" is certainly fresher and more natural than the bulk of the art of his time, but it must be said that a good deal of its freshness and naturalness is due to a certain *naïveté* of incompetence rather than to simplicity of mind. For Rousseau as a composer was by no means an accomplished craftsman. Rameau once said of his music that, while some pieces showed the hand of a master, others revealed the ignorance of a schoolboy—a statement that sums up "Le Devin du Village," which is as full of melodies that have the delightful spontaneity of folk-songs as it is of crudities and technical awkwardness. Rousseau, whose musical equipment had been acquired by the copying of music for a livelihood and by an intense love and desultory study of the art continually thwarted by the other preoccupations of his genius, could do no more than dabble in it all his life. But that he never ceased to worship it is proved by his collection of about a hundred pieces and songs to which, late in life, he gave the title of "Consolations des Misères de ma Vie."

The plot of "Le Devin du Village," a typical though very innocent eighteenth-century intrigue, is as simple as possible. It turns around three characters: the shepherd Colin, the shepherdess Colette, and a personage who enjoys the reputation of Village Soothsayer. The latter is ap-

JEAN-JACQUES ROUSSEAU AFTER A POSTEL BY LA TOUR, 1753.

proached by Colette, who appeals to him for help in restoring her faithless lover to her. Colin's new bond is merely one of interest, and the supposed Soothsayer, whose art in reality only lies in his wisdom and kindliness, pretends to read in a magic book that Colette in her turn has found a new attraction. She falls in with the stratagem, and jealousy does the rest in bringing back her erring swain.

The piece soon became popular and received its first public performance at the Académie Royale de Musique in Paris on March 1st, 1753. Here its curious and circuitous career opened. The philosopher's plot was next taken up by an actress, the charming and virtuous Madame Favart, who turned it into what she called a parody, but what in reality was a simple little ballad-opera on popular airs, one of them actually borrowed from Rousseau's work. It follows the original plot in all its essentials, and parody is limited to the transcription of the lyrics into a quaint country dialect. The new piece, entitled "Les Amours de Bastien et Bastienne," was produced by the *Comédiens Italiens Ordinaires du Roi* on September 26th, 1753, Madame Favart herself playing the part of Bastienne. She was the first actress who dared to appear on the stage in the part of a country girl clad in a realistic costume, without the hoops, powder, towering head-gear and diamonds that seemed indispensable to a public who liked to have both vice and innocence wrapped up in decorous and graceful artifice. But her hold on even the most sophisticated was strong enough for her to venture to brave the storm of protest that broke over her head, which she had the audacity to expose with no other adornment than her own hair.

It was Madame Favart's version that found its way to Vienna in 1768, at a time when a little boy of twelve named Wolfgang Amadeus Mozart had just made the acquaintance of Dr. Messmer* and his wife, who had built a small amateur theatre. The child, who wished to compose a little opera for them, seized eagerly on the almost literal German translation by Friedrich Wilhelm Weiskern, and so " Bastien und Bastienne " came into the world. It is naturally a somewhat primitive work, yet the boy scores over both the philosopher and the actress. When it comes to an opera, the child of twelve is less ingenuous than the author of the " Confessions " and the shrewd woman of the stage.

A comparison between Rousseau's and Mozart's works (Madame Favart's version is of no significance musically) is in almost every particular favourable to the latter. There are amazingly few signs of immaturity in the boy's score, whereas the music of the man of forty at once reveals the fact that maturity was altogether

* Or Mesmer, the originator of mesmerism.

beyond his reach. In Mozart there is a sure sense of dramatic situation and of climax ; in Rousseau we find simply amiable music fitted, and sometimes badly fitted, to an amiable libretto. Even in purely technical matters, the young Mozart stands head and shoulders above the elderly Rousseau. His harmony is much fuller, and his part-writing, with its elegant and adroit little contrapuntal devices here and there, makes Rousseau's workmanship look all the more clumsy in comparison. Again, the boy handles the orchestra with much greater skill ; his transparent blending of colour is delightful and his love of detail induces him to write out the parts with meticulous care, while the man's score shows a haphazard and perfunctory notation : his phrasing is slipshod and his dynamic intentions often doubtful, such remarks as *fort*, *doux* and *demi jeu* being scattered more or less casually through the score. Though both composers use very few wind instruments, the boy gives them far more independent and therefore more important parts. In Rousseau's work, with very few exceptions, they merely double the strings, and he seems to be afraid of combining them frequently with the singing voice, for they are confined for the most part to the purely instrumental numbers such as the overture, the dances and the interludes. There is scarcely any climax in the philosopher's opera, which ends with a kind of *divertissement* of songs and dances that has nothing to do with the plot, while Mozart's score contains more than a germ of a concerted *finale :* a duet of far greater dimensions than any of the preceding numbers, followed without a break by a final *ensemble* for the three characters.

For one or two charming things in " Bastien and Bastienne," which are not to be found in " Le Devin du Village," Madame Favart is responsible. Colas, the Soothsayer, in her version performs the feat of " singing to his bagpipe," and in Mozart's work he makes his first entry to the sound of that instrument imitated in a delicious little pastoral movement for strings on a drone bass and with the humorously realistic touch of a G sharp in the key of D major. And his conjuring aria, with its ridiculous jargon, comes from the same source. In Rousseau's opera, the conjuring scene goes on pantomimically to mildly bucolic music that has no shadow of characterization in it, while Mozart's aria has an extraordinarily dramatic and comic effect that foreshadows his maturest period. In the whole of his work, we can trace a distinct striving after character ; and there are many tense moments, always tempered by the spirit of comedy, that are strikingly prophetic of his greatest work.

Rousseau's knowledge of the resources of each instrument was evidently very limited. He is extremely shy of string effects like the *pizzicato* and the *tremolo*. His harmony is shabby and he is too frequently content with leaving it to the mercy of the harpsichord player, many of his arias being scored merely for violins in unison with an unfigured bass. Mozart, on the contrary, leaves nothing to chance. In one particular, however, Rousseau is superior : his recitative is more expressive and more individual than that of Mozart. He is, in fact, very careful to lift it to a higher function than that of simply forming a modulative bridge from one number to another ; and there are elaborate expression marks such as *ironie et dépit*, *menace*, *douleur tendre* and *réflexion triste*, which show a desire to infuse some dramatic significance into the *secco* recitative.

There is no spoken dialogue in " Le Devin du Village," the whole work is composed through ; whereas in " Bastien and Bastienne," curiously enough, the first few numbers are linked up by recitatives, which are then suddenly dropped half-way through the score and replaced by dialogue. Mozart employs no chorus, but in Rousseau's work there is a very fresh, bright choral number—one of the best pieces in the score—that rounds off the plot admirably before the irrelevant *divertissement* begins.

" Le Devin du Village " would have to be very much touched up before it could be given the chance of a successful revival. Already in

1828, until which time it dragged out a spasmodic existence, it was consigned to oblivion by a malicious humorist—Berlioz was suspected—who threw a large powdered wig on the stage. Nor could any amount of retouching impart vitality to it, since the process would probably efface the innocence that is its only engaging quality. The work is still worth studying at the piano, however, for the real melodic charm of many of the numbers, for a few characteristic touches here and there, and for the clean pastoral feeling which is perhaps all the more refreshing because it is so amateurish. There are passages that make us think of the frail and tender grace of Couperin, and the work recalls many other charming things in the eighteenth-century music of France, for in spite of the author's abusive "Lettre sur la Musique Française" and his siding with the Italians in the *guerre des bouffons*, the work is as French as possible. It has been compared to the French painting of the period, but it has hardly the delightful preciosity of the school as a whole. A certain honesty about it makes it akin to the warm-hearted reality, though not the brilliant technique, of Chardin rather than the *fêtes galantes* of Watteau or the elegant allegories of Boucher.

After Mozart's setting, Rousseau's subject seems to have found rest, but his music lingered on. In France, many of the songs and dances became extremely popular ; and one of the melodies, oddly enough, found its way into England* in the form of a hymn long known as "Rousseau's Dream," on which Cramer wrote some variations in the early part of the nineteenth century. One of the tunes is still to be heard daily, played by the *carillon* in one of the steeples of Geneva, Rousseau's birthplace.

The philosopher's opera was killed by the wig incident in Paris : the actress's effort was never more than an ephemeral success ; and it is the little boy's work alone that survives.

* No doubt by way of Dr. Burney's adaptation, produced at Drury Lane, under the title of "The Cunning Man," in 1766.

IV. "TOM JONES" ON THE FRENCH STAGE

IV. "TOM JONES" ON THE FRENCH STAGE

ONE of the perversions of the French upper classes after the peace with England of 1763—the most harmless one, surely, yet not without its share in the conditions which eventually exasperated the populace into revolution—was Anglomania. Cultured Parisian society affected the sports and fashions of London, the very vocabulary became seasoned with Anglicisms, and English literature was widely read. Fielding's "Tom Jones" was a favourite book, and the impression made by its broad humanity and unvarnished truth was the deeper, perhaps, by contrast with the excessive formality and artificiality in a dire reaction against which the country was soon to be involved. On February 27th, 1765, the hero of Fielding's work, accompanied by several of the chief characters, appeared on the French stage in the shape of a feeble libretto by the notoriously ignorant and gullible Antoine Alexandre Henri Poinsinet, and clothed with delightful music by François-André Danican Philidor, one of the creators of French comic opera in company with Grétry, Monsigny and Duni, but even more famous in his time as an unapproachable chess player. The book was such an ineffectual travesty of the story, and presented such a sorry portrait of its protagonist that the opera, in spite of its delicious and no doubt at that time rather astonishing music, was ignominiously hissed off the stage. Poinsinet had succeeded in robbing the novel of all its racy flavour, in giving the intrigue the most insipid turn, and in making of Tom Jones himself—human, all-too-human creature of flesh and blood that he is—the pasteboard figure of a puppet show. The dull librettist, who imperilled more than one opera of Philidor's in his time, seems to have worked much on the same principle as Joseph Reed, by whom another opera on the subject appeared in London that year, and who says in his preface, "I have stripp'd the hero of his libertinism to render him, as I imagined, more amiable and interesting," adding this characteristic touch, "and have metamorphos'd Parson Supple into a country 'squire to avoid giving offence to the cloth."* Reed's version has, at any rate, the merit of preserving as much as possible of Fielding's own dialogue ; for the rest, it is no better than that of Poinsinet, from which it actually borrows the idea of legitimizing Tom, as the author freely confesses, while he emphasizes the fact

* Reed's "Tom Jones" was performed at Covent Garden in 1769, with music by Abel, Arne, Arnold, Bach (undoubtedly Johann Christian, since the name appears as "Mr. Bach"), Baildon, Boyce, Corelli, Galuppi, Granom, Handel, Hasse, Holcombe, van Maldore, Pergolesi, and including such popular songs as "Sir Roger de Coverley," "The Roast Beef of Old England," "Sir Simon the King," and "Old King Cole."

that two acts of his work were already finished when the French version fell into his hands.

One reads not without glee of the defeat of Poinsinet's libretto, a libel on Fielding, whose great and deeply human novel is cut down to suit the surface decorum of a nobility and gentry that liked to see virtue triumphant on the stage and in its own immediate family circle, if not beyond. Poinsinet draws everything exceedingly mild. Jones, perfectly immaculate, is merely mistaken for a rake, and a very harmless one at that, by a clumsily-contrived stage situation ; Western, although more true to his prototype, is much toned down ; Lady Bellaston is suppressed, and Molly Seagrim totally ignored. But Poinsinet is not guilty of tameness and excessive punctilio alone ; he persistently neglects countless opportunities for high comedy, and indulges in some deplorable verses, such as this :

> " A ton nom seul, ô mon cher Jone [*sic*]
> Je sens mon cœur qui m'abandonne."

But what was to be expected of an author whose name was proverbial for stupidity, and whose ignorance, credulity and presumption continually made him the butt of his waggish contemporaries? It was Poinsinet—to recall but one of the numerous stories which illustrate his dupability—who, on being told that he was elected to fill a lucrative post at St. Petersburg, applied himself to a serious study of what he believed to be Russian, only to discover at the end of six months that he had been made to learn low Breton.

In spite of its failure, the opera reappeared less than a year later (January 30th, 1766) in a revised version from which the most glaring incongruities of the libretto had been expunged. It was now received with enthusiasm by the Parisians, and made its way as far as Dresden, whither it was taken by the "French Court Comedians" the same year.

Philidor did not begin to write operas, or indeed to compose seriously, until the age of thirty-three, five years after his return from England in 1754, when several of his friends, including Diderot, entreated him not to neglect his remarkable musical gifts entirely in favour of his passion for chess. Before 1759, when "Blaise le Savetier" was staged at the Théatre de la Foire St. Laurent, he had practised music in a desultory manner. Even as a boy, when he was page in the King's Music and studied under Campra, his attention was more readily attracted by his favourite game, which he challenged several courtiers to play against him. In spite of the encouragement Louis XV gave him when he had composed a motet at the age of fifteen, he left Court at nineteen and undertook a journey to Holland and Germany, where he defeated the greatest chess players of the age. Staying at

FRONTISPIECE TO PHILIDOR'S "ANALYSE DU JEU DES ECHECS."

Aix-la-Chapelle in 1748 to write his " Analyse du Jeu des Echecs," he was invited by Lord Sandwich to visit the English camp between Maestricht and Bois-le-Duc, where the Duke of Cumberland induced him to go to London. Here he settled down for several years, publishing his book in 1749. Fielding's " Tom Jones " appearing that same year, it is by no means unlikely that Philidor should have then and there become acquainted with the subject of his later opera.

To know the history of the earlier half of Philidor's life is to suspect him, not unreasonably, of being little more than a dabbler in an art that ranked but second in his affections, or, at best, to expect to trace in his music the coldly calculating mind of the chess player. On opening a score of his for the first time it is scarcely unnatural that one should be prepared to meet, if not with something exceedingly flimsy, then at least with something rather dull and lacking in spontaneity. How surprising then is the discovery of music that is not only finer in quality than that of Philidor's fellow-composers of French comic opera—not excepting even Grétry—but music that has intrinsic charms which the passing of time has not paled into insignificance. In place of the shoddy workmanship which the curious investigator may pardonably look for, he will be astonished to find a sound, closely-knit texture, full and varied harmony, firm, nervy counterpoint with inner parts full of life and basses far from rigid, and an instrumentation that is bold, colourful and always telling. True, there is little individuality or originality ; the music has a kind of natural vigour rather than genuine dramatic power, effect rather than emotion. It is the sort of music propelled by the composer's energy and joy in his task rather than produced by the stimulation of his feelings—music of the senses, not of the heart. It exhilarates, but does not touch. Philidor had more accomplishment than education and wit, or, as M. de Laborde, Groom of the Privy Chamber to the King, said, one doubts whether kindly or cruelly, on hearing him utter some particularly fatuous inanities, " He has no common sense, he is all genius." But why not, if we fail to find great human truth in his music, enjoy it for what it is worth ? It has good points enough to tickle our palate, and though it cannot nourish and sustain, it will prove more than sufficient for the need of the hour.

Philidor deserves neither the almost unheard-of popularity he enjoyed as composer of some two dozen operas during the latter half of his life, nor the abuse of some of his contemporaries, who accused him of shameless plagiarism,* " vicious

* This almost indelible reproach had its origin in a remarkable likeness between an air in " Le Sorcier " (1764) and one in Gluck's " Orfeo," which may well be accepted as accidental since it cannot be conclusively proved that Philidor must have known Gluck's work at that time.

prosody," and all manner of technical shortcomings. Gluck's judgment of his music, " It is a watch enriched by a few jewels, but with a worthless interior mechanism," is certainly unjust. For proof we need only glance at the Overture to " Tom Jones," which is representative of the whole opera. Jewels there are none ; it is plain music without superfluous detail, but its inner workings are sound and neat, and they fit to perfection. The overture is not in the Lully form with its slow introduction, but plunges straight into a vigorous, joyous *allegro*. There is little attempt to create an atmosphere appropriate to Fielding's work even as attenuated in Poinsinet's libretto, just as there is scarcely any delineation of character throughout the opera, unless we accept the elaborate and interesting horn passages as a hint at Squire Western's hunting proclivities. But although the overture be irrelevant in detail, its general mood is perfectly in the picture. It generalizes, yet remains applicable to what is to follow, not unlike one of the introductory chapters which preface each section of Fielding's novel—one might say, perhaps, the one headed, " Containing matter accommodated to every taste," for is not the Overture too fresh and gladsome to displease anyone, and too little expressive of a distinct personality to jar on any temperament ?

That Philidor was an innovator not without

audacity can be gathered from his splendid orchestration, a curious instance of which may be quoted from Western's great hunting song, which has sustained harmonics in all the string parts, not excepting the double basses ; from the combination of two contrasting themes in some of the duets, the stirring unaccompanied fugal drinking song, the interesting parts assigned to the orchestral basses, always alive and moving and often embellished with little expressive figures, the finely shaped septet, which makes quite an important finale to the second act ; and from several other remarkable features. One could go on drawing attention to many a surprising modulation here, a bold syncopation there, a touch of colour hardly to be expected from the limited orchestra* elsewhere. There are charmingly mixed rhythms in the first duet between Sophia and Honour ; some delicious episodes in the rondo in which the latter imitates Tom's love song ; great beauty of line, liveliness of detail and graceful interlacing of parts in Tom's great air ; some effective if rather mild dramatic touches in the duet between Sophia and Western ; and some splendidly expressive phrases in Sophia's long, varied and fully accompanied recitative—the only one in the opera. The voices in the numerous concerted pieces are invariably well interwoven.

* The opera is scored for oboes, bassoons, horns and strings.

"TOM JONES"

It is to be regretted that Philidor seems to have neglected an opportunity for descriptive music given him by his librettist, who, at the opening of the third act says, "The symphony of the *entr'acte* depicts a night." It would have been interesting to know his treatment of such an interlude, but no trace of it is to be found in the score.

Concessions to convention are sufficiently rare in this opera, but only a composer of greater originality could have avoided them altogether. The work ends, for instance, with a *vaudeville*,* a tune sung in turn by all the chief characters, each to a different verse. This indulgence in a fashionable device is unworthy of the rest of the opera, for although calculated to send the hearer home contentedly humming, it fails to make a fit climax to the whole. There is much also that is artificial and baroque, and especially vexing is the frequency of the stiff pattern of the *da capo* aria, so inimical to dramatic truth. That Philidor was not entirely free from Italian influence may be judged from an air of Honour's, a conventional soubrette song in 6-8 time of the type that flourishes in Cimarosa and Pergolesi, and reaches its culmination in Despina's songs in "Così fan tutte."

As the opera goes on, although not abating

* A more familiar example of the *vaudeville* occurs at the end of Mozart's "Seraglio."

in quality, it becomes a little monotonous, for Philidor, in spite of the fact that his invention remains charming throughout, is incapable of evolving enough new and contrasting matter to sustain the interest to the end. As the first delighted surprise wears off, his inability to outline living human beings grows a little too glaringly apparent. But where is the work that has not its defects? If there be one in this world that leaves one entirely uncritical, it is "Figaro," and precisely with that "Tom Jones" has at least one delightful feature in common—its music is contemporary with its subject. It will therefore always remain, whatever else it may lack, a perfect and engaging artistic reflection of its period. Viewing Philidor's "Tom Jones" in that light, we might almost be tempted to extend to it the prophecy of Gibbon—already half fulfilled—that Fielding's work would survive the Palace of the Escurial and the Imperial Eagle of the house of Austria.

V. A MISJUDGED COMPOSER

V. A MISJUDGED COMPOSER

AMONG the figures in musical history who are remembered by their shortcomings alone, the most pathetic, because the most unjustly treated, is surely Niccolo Piccinni, who, had he not had the misfortune of coming into conflict with Gluck, would certainly have established for himself a reputation, not comparable to that of the greatest masters, but at any rate not inferior to that of many other important composers who have contributed to the making of opera. Piccinni is regarded by the musical historian as one of those insignificant musicians who tried to work up by intrigue a reputation which their work was too feeble to secure for them, and who richly deserve the obscurity and ill-fame into which they have sunk. The truth about Piccinni is considered as definitely established, and it is commonly thought unnecessary to enquire into the circumstances of his career or look at his work ; it is calmly taken for granted that he must have been a wretched composer, since he was defeated by Gluck, and it does not seem to occur to anyone that there is just a chance of his being scarcely less good than, but simply different from, Gluck. A study of his operas reveals the fact that they are certainly inferior to Gluck's masterpieces, but that, on the whole, there is plenty of evidence of genius about them. It is paying Gluck a poor compliment to assume that the man he conquered must have been a weakling. On the other hand, it says a good deal for Piccinni that he should have been compared at all, and by a large faction favourably compared, to the great reformer.

An impartial study of the vast literature that deals with the violent strife between the Gluckists and the Piccinnists, removes the widespread notion that the Italian composer was a jealous and crafty schemer. The fact is that he stood entirely aloof from the contest, that he was a modest, peace-loving and retiring man, who asked no more than a fair hearing and was quite content to let others make their reputation for themselves by whatever means they chose. In this respect, Piccinni is a more sympathetic personality than Gluck, who was not reluctant to take an active share in the war of pamphlets and libels that raged in Paris and caused a revolution in intellectual circles, which was only quelled by the outbreak of a political upheaval of far greater significance.

But however inoffensive and attractive Piccinni may have been as a man, posterity must judge him by his work alone. And it is here that posterity has been most unjust to him. To form an equitable judgment, it is necessary to begin by forgetting the historical accident that brought Piccinni into rivalry with Gluck. It was a mere caprice of fate that threw an Italian and a German composer together on the Parisian stage, and involved them in the fierce struggle which a frivolous and highly cultured society was only too ready to wage on their behalf. The contest was the more absurd because the two composers were sufficiently dissimilar for people to admire the good qualities of both. They might have appreciated at once the tragic grandeur of Gluck and the vivacity and adroitness of Piccinni, and the same hearer might have condemned the former's angularity and monotony and the latter's lack of great inspiration.

There is no doubt that Gluck is the greater composer of the two ; but why should not Piccinni's merits be recognized even though they are overshadowed by a more highly gifted genius ? We might as well refuse to enjoy the " Barbiere " because of the existence of the " Meistersinger."

The Italian composer, though intellectually and artistically inferior to the German, was at any rate a better craftsman. Piccinni wrote with a remarkable, indeed with a fatal, facility. A complete list of his operas* contains no less than 139 dramatic works, of which the first was only written in his twenty-seventh year. This was " Le Donne Dispettose," produced at Naples in 1755. In 1761 alone he wrote six operas, having produced at Rome the previous year, " La Cecchina, ossia La Buona Figliuola," which,

* *Rivista Musicale Italiana.* Vol. 8 (1901), p. 75.

in spite of the fact that Logroscino's comic operas then monopolized the stage, had a greater vogue than any other *opera buffa* ever written, and was given for years on every Italian stage and in most of the principal European centres.

An examination of the score of " La Cecchina " reveals little more than a faithful adherence to the mannerisms of the period. Every phrase, every harmonic turn, is in the Italian manner of the eighteenth century, and might have been written by any save two or three of the most original composers of the time. Piccinni certainly is no salient personality, and he was avowedly opposed to innovation.

Nevertheless, this opera is replete with a fluency and vivacity that is quite in the best vein of the comic opera of the period, whose stereotyped patterns are almost forgotten in the enjoyment of their melodic charm. It is mellifluous, pretty music, written without any great care to fit it to the stage situation, yet with more of that care than the public of the time, who simply wanted to hear agreeable music, ever expected. There is some delightful harmony and surprising modulation in this little opera, besides occasional attempts to create dramatic effect by means of tremolos and other conventional tricks; but Piccinni fails as yet to infuse real force into a regularly developed movement, and the action is generally sacrificed to the exigencies of musical form. There is only a rudimentary *finale*, simply a duet rounding off the uninterrupted chain of arias that forms the opera, and the orchestra is not reinforced to create a culminating point; it is mainly limited to strings, although earlier in the work two flutes and two horns are used once or twice. Orchestral effects are almost entirely absent, but there is an amusing aria that recalls one in Mozart's "La finta giardiniera," where various instruments are exhorted to play for a dance. These instruments, however, are not there: the trumpets referred to in the libretto are replaced by horns, the violins imitate drum-rolls as best they can, and guitars are suggested by *pizzicato* strings.

The following year (1761), Piccinni had a great success with "L'Olimpiade," which had been previously set to music by Leonardo Leo, Pergolesi, Galuppi and Jommelli, whose versions were all eclipsed by his own.

It would be impossible to deal with all the operas of the Italian period in detail; they follow each other in rapid succession and show little development in the composer's outlook. The great change in Piccinni's life as well as in his music came about in 1776, when he was called to Paris in order to save the Opera from ruin. He arrived there with his family in the course of a bitter winter, and his discomfort was intensified by the fact that he did not know a word of French. A painful process of acquiring the language under the guidance of Marmontel resulted in his being able to set it to music before he could speak it. The first French opera was " Roland," produced at the Académie Royale de Musique on January 27th, 1778, and dedicated to the young Queen Marie-Antoinette.* The feud between the respective admirers of Gluck and Piccinni had already begun,† for the latter's Italian operas were not unknown in Paris. Piccinni himself was anxious to keep out of the quarrel ; he went his own way, and his timid nature was almost overwhelmed by the opposition he met with at the Opera. Actors, chorus, orchestra, all were already on the side of Gluck, who was the one man capable of making them emerge from the sloth into which the stage had sunk at that time.‡

Marmontel was the author of the libretto of " Roland," and when it was performed for the first time, privately at his wedding, the poet exclaimed: " The success of this work, which seems to me infallible, must end the quarrel ! " It did nothing of the kind: the contest grew

* Piccinni succeeded Gluck as her singing master.

† In October, 1777, Madame Riccoboni wrote to Garrick: " People tear each other's eyes out for or against Gluck."

‡ Rousseau's amusing description of the state of affairs at the Opera would be dismissed as incredible were it not confirmed by Ginguené and others.

more violent than ever and went on unabated for several years.

Society was divided. The subject was not safe. Men met each other for the first time with the threatening question: " Sir, are you a Gluckist or a Piccinnist? " Quarrels and duels over the two composers and the ideals attributed to them were of daily occurrence.

There is a remarkable change of style in " Roland "; the composer's feeling for French opera as distinct from Italian is very striking, and his striving after dramatic truth becomes evident. Since Italian opera of the period was more alive and natural than French opera prior to the reforms introduced by Gluck, there can be no doubt that Piccinni, who had now made a considerable stride forward, must himself have been largely influenced by the German master, a fact that dismisses for good and all the idea that Piccinni set out to defeat Gluck's principles. Had not the war between their partisans begun before the production of " Roland," the two composers would never have come into conflict at all.

There is an elegant and chivalric, if not a heroic feeling about this first French work of Piccinni's. Its most striking feature is an unmistakable likeness to Mozart's " Idomeneo," which was certainly written under its influence, and comes much nearer in spirit to Piccinni than to Gluck, who is generally supposed to be its godfather.*

After " Roland " came a series of other tragic operas, which all show a distinct advance on Piccinni's Italian style, and a progress in themselves. The recitative becomes more alive and true to the dramatic situation. It is always fully scored and frequently introduces short thematic fragments that underline the dramatic situation. In the arias there is little overloaded and false *coloratura*, and the *finale*, usually a chorus with intermittent passages for the soloists, assumes more and more the character of a true climax. The orchestration is fuller, and there is a tendency to create greater variety by the use of horns in thematic passages, the introduction of dramatic effects by means of tremolos and other tentative devices. Concerted numbers become more frequent, but they are still rather formal and too often arrest the action instead of hastening it forward to a culmination, as they do in Mozart. The choral numbers show some delightful part-writing and comparatively seldom proceed in blocks of chords. In his ballet music, that superflous appendix which the Paris Opera has not seen fit to remove even yet, Piccinni is less happy. He disliked dancing and wrote dance music under constraint; but he was too

* The young Mozart must have heard " Roland " during his stay in Paris in 1778. " Idomeneo " was written in 1780.

weak to insist on the removal of this utterly false convention, which even the despotic Gluck, whose works clearly reveal his intense aversion to it, was unable either to discard or to fit appropriately into his Greek tragedies.

Piccinni's care for detail, his descriptive passages in the recitative and the variety of his moods increase in his later works. In "Atys," the dramatic feeling becomes really stirring at times and the minor close of the *finale*, which is in a major key, is a touch of originality by no means without daring for the time. In "Iphigénie en Tauride," set to the same text as Gluck's opera, there is some very fine tempest music, and the work shows dramatic feeling not only in the *motion* of the musical texture, but in the *harmony*. This work, in spite of Gluck's superior success, was fairly well received, but on the second night Mlle. Laguerre came on the stage intoxicated, and drew from Sophie Arnould, the famous witticism: "C'est Iphigénie en Champagne."

"Didon," the last French opera before the composer's retreat to Italy at the outbreak of the Revolution, has more contrast than any of the preceding works, but it proves that an artist's uncontrolled emotion—the opera was written in fits of weeping—does not always fully emerge in his work.

In the less important comic operas of the French period, Piccinni very wisely reverts to his early Italian style and dispenses with recitative. "Le Faux Lord"* is a delicious little work that still preserves a good deal of its freshness.

It is time to discard the current fiction of Piccinni's intrigues against Gluck, to whose memory after his death he was anxious to institute an annual concert, and to whom he said that the French stage owed as much as it did to Corneille. Musical history has too long looked upon him as an insignificant charlatan, and he ought at last to be recognized as what he really was: a composer who in all sincerity contributed a modest but by no means negligible share to the development of opera, and a sympathetic personality who deserves to be delivered from the false position into which he has been thrust by perfunctory historians.

* The score in the British Museum is a most interesting document, bearing traces of the French Revolution: the references to royalty on the title page are carefully obliterated. It also bears the composer's autograph signature, which should remove all doubt as to the spelling of his name.

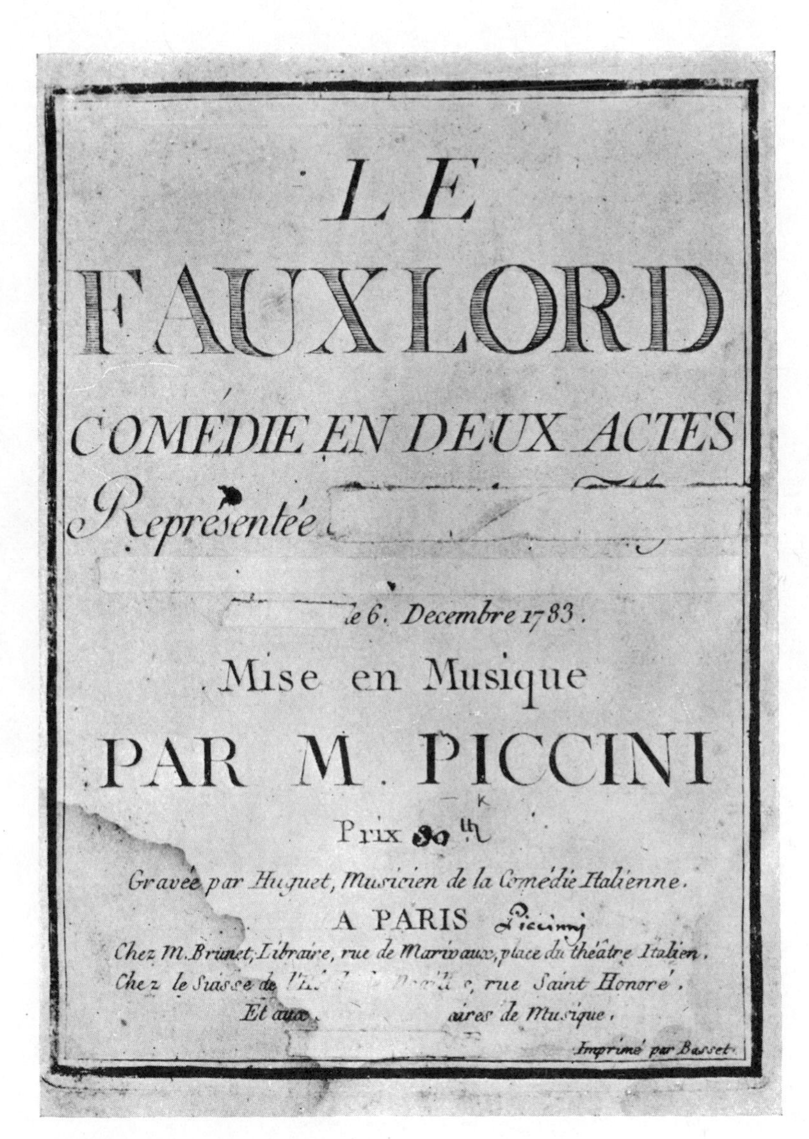

LE

FAUXLORD

COMÉDIE EN DEUX ACTES

Représentée [illegible]

[illegible] le 6. Decembre 1783.

Mise en Musique

PAR M. PICCINI

Prix [illegible]

Gravée par Huguet, Musicien de la Comédie Italienne.

A PARIS

Chez M. Brunet, Libraire, rue de Marivaux, place du théâtre Italien.

Chez le Suisse de l'H[illegible] rue Saint Honoré.

Et aux [illegible] aires de Musique.

Imprimé par Basset.

TITLE PAGE OF THE SCORE AT THE BRITISH MUSEUM.

VI. AN ERROR OF ROSSINI'S YOUTH

VI. AN ERROR OF ROSSINI'S YOUTH

IN 1807, a bright, spirited boy of fifteen, of defective education, but full of natural intelligence, for the first time entered a building at Bologna, which he little dreamt would one day bear his name inscribed over its portals—the institution now known as the *Liceo Rossini.* He was even then no novice in the art to which he was going to devote his life (until the day he chose to forsake it almost wholly for epicurism), for had he not already written, among other things, a number of songs for his mother, baker's daughter and *prima donna buffa*; little pieces for two horns for himself and his father, once town trumpeter at Pesaro and now reduced to playing the horn at the theatres up and down the country at which his wife made her spasmodic appearances; an opera, "Demetrio," for the remarkable Mombelli family, the mother of which wrote the libretto while her children took the parts; and a Mass for male voices for a church at Ravenna? Small wonder that the precocious lad did not relish the counterpoint class of a Padre Mattei, who could give no better reason for certain things in music being permissible or inadmissible than the fact that "They are the rule." Small wonder, likewise, that this same clerical pedant had but a poor opinion of a child whose musical education had begun under a master who played scales on the piano with first finger and thumb, and combined his music-teaching with the sale of spirits—a child who had the effrontery to write church music without knowing anything about counterpoint, and was devoid, as it soon became apparent, of any aptitude for acquiring such knowledge. Thus, with young Rossini continually chafing and questioning, with old Mattei always checking enquiry by stating the authority of usage, the lessons were barren enough. Not so the violoncello tuition of Cavedagni, whose class the boy joined shortly after his admission to the institution. Here his progress was astonishingly rapid, for wherever it was a question of solving a problem by dexterity rather than by learning, nothing was troublesome to the budding composer, who all his life remained an artist better acquainted with the expedients of his craft than with its science, and could dispense with the latter because of his skilful handling of the former. Before long, the youth was able to take part in the performance of a Haydn Quartet, and very little later he could grapple with Mozart's violoncello parts. Great was his joy in these two masters, whom he worshipped to such an extent that his fellow-students dubbed him *il tedeschino*—the little German. Not unnaturally at his age—he was now seventeen—admiration led to emulation, and soon his first String Quartet was finished and followed by four others. There is no documentary evidence that more than one of the five Quartets was written in 1809, but from the similarity of their style and their equal immaturity, it may be safely assumed that they all belong approximately to the same period.

It was about this time that Rossini wrote his first Cantata, "Il pianto d'armonia per la morte d'Orfeo," which won him a prize at the *Liceo*. At this time, too, he took to conducting an orchestra, called the *Accademia dei Concerti*, for which he re-scored a number of quartets by Haydn and Mozart—proof enough that he had no real feeling for quartet-writing as a medium of expression that relies mainly on contour, and cannot be replaced at will by another whose chief characteristic is colour. And if further evidence be required that he did not understand the peculiar disposition of tissues of a combination of four singl-string instruments, his own Quartets furnish it abundantly enough. But though he was unconscious of his deficiency in the direction of texture, several indications show that he cannot have been unaware of his defective counterpoint. There is the tale of his Overture in fugal style, modelled on that to the "Magic Flute," which he destroyed of his own accord after trying it over with his orchestra; and there is the story of his parting with Mattei after ascertaining from the scholarly *abbate* that he knew enough of counterpoint to write operas, which was all he desired to do.

The String Quartets, Rossini's only deviation into the domain of chamber music still extant, are the work of an amateur in the literal as well as the current sense of the term—the labour of love of an ardent and inexperienced youth—all the more attractive perhaps for being clumsily executed. Adolphe Adam* once said that amateur music seemed to be composed for the happiness of those who play it and for the despair of those who listen to it. The first half of this epigram no doubt applies to the youthful Rossini and his friends, whose delight in performing his new Quartets must have been intense; but whether these works are calculated to drive the hearer into a frenzy of irritation must at least remain open to doubt until they have been either heard or at least read through. A performance is not likely to take place nowadays until some publisher with more enterprise than business instinct re-issues them, for they have long been out of print; and no quartet association can perhaps be expected to be sufficiently disinterested to have a set of parts copied out at the British Museum in order to gratify the curiosity of a handful of antiquarians. Nor would they do the composer himself a great service, for he had a poor opinion of these early works of his in later

* *Souvenirs d'un Musicien*, p. 221.

years, and they were published, according to Fétis, against his wish. They came out in London, in parts only, about 1824, under the following pompous title-page: "Cinque Quartetti Originali per due Violini, Viola e Violoncello, Composti dal Celebre Rossini, e dall' Editore Ricordi dedicati a S. E. Lord Burghersh, Ministro di S. M. Britannica in Toscana. Londra, presso Grua e Ricordi, 2 Albemarle Street, Piccadilly."

All the five Quartets are in major keys (G, A, B flat, E flat and D), and each has three movements, the middle movement being invariably a short Andante, the finale, with one exception, a Rondo. In the first movements a strict sonata form is, of course, everywhere maintained, and altogether the Quartets give the impression of having been cut to pattern. There is great facility of thematic invention in every movement: the music flows on gracefully and elegantly, but without a trace of individuality. The influence of Haydn and Mozart is obvious at every turn, the former predominating. This fact need not, however, be attributed to any preference for Haydn on the part of the composer, who later in life said that Mozart stood absolutely alone in music; it is simply due to the circumstance that Haydn's more loosely-knit method of quartet writing was the one which Rossini could hope to imitate with a certain measure of success. His Quartets, in fact, suffer from exactly the same defect as Haydn's, though naturally in a far greater degree owing to his inexperience: their part-writing is ill-balanced. The melodic line is nearly always entrusted to the first violin, the other parts being kept comparatively idle, reduced to playing uninteresting accompaniments. The music, in consequence, is top-heavy. It is true that the lower instruments sometimes take a prominent part, but they never do so in a truly contrapuntal manner: it is invariably one single part that stands out; each instrument politely waits for the other to recede before it attempts to say something of moment.

But the music has its redeeming features. Even where the mere texture is concerned, there is something to be said in its favour; for, although Rossini's quartet-writing is bad, his writing for each individual string instrument is excellent, already showing clearly that gift of stating even the simplest phrase in the most effective manner possible, a talent undreamt of in the Italy of his days, where instrumental values were totally neglected in favour of vocal perfection. Rossini's feeling for colour is already in evidence here: the Finale from the fourth Quartet, for instance, has a *sul ponticello* effect in the first violin part.

As regards form, the Quartets present nothing new. Conventional bricks, neatly trimmed enough, are pieced together into a safe and sound edifice devoid of all originality. The harmony is a little more interesting, for there are occasional traces of the bold modulations which still astonish us in the operas of Rossini, if we compare them with other Italian dramatic works of his time, and here and there we come across unexpected chromatic notes that suddenly enliven a whole passage, although they are carefully confined to a single part, the other three instruments not daring to sideslip while their partner indulges in so perilous an escapade. The chromatic accents in the slow movement of the first Quartet, the enharmonic modulation in the Andante of the third, and the extraordinary, almost Schubertian plunge into a remote key just before the close of the last, are all strides into the future, the composer's own and music's generally, unconscious on his part, but nevertheless significant.

Rossini's own instrument, the violoncello, is occasionally treated with especial care—as in the finale of the first Quartet, the initial movement of the second, and the slow movement of the third, with its fine dramatic declamatory opening. The future operatic composer peeps out in this passage, and more particularly in the rather superficially elegiac Andante of the second Quartet. But on the whole there is little to be found that savours strongly of Rossini, although the opening movement of the last quartet has a little of his demeanour, and the sauntering dotted rhythm of the Finale is distinctly characteristic of him; generally the *tedeschino* in him is uppermost. The gaiety of the Rondo of the second Quartet, for instance, is the good-natured Austrian humour of Haydn, not the Italian effervescence and sprightliness of Rossini himself. And thus we meet Haydn and Mozart, diluted for the most part, all along. But in spite of immaturity, flimsy technique, and lack of individuality, these quartets have at any rate the natural flow, the high spirits, and the impeccable taste we love in much of the later Rossini. He never again swerved from the true path assigned to him, and since this one *faux pas* of his was committed in the flush of youthful enthusiasm, and not without grace, it may be readily forgiven him.

VII. CHERUBINI IN CHURCH

VII. CHERUBINI IN CHURCH

IN 1808 Cherubini abandoned the composition of operas to which he had devoted himself with an almost incredible energy; the whirlpool ot Parisian musical life had at last thrown him into a state of nervous depression to which his gloomy and pessimistic nature had always been prone. A period of rest, enlivened by painting and the study of botany, was concluded by a visit to the Prince de Chimay at his castle in Belgium, and it was there that, for the first time since the days of his youth, Cherubini was prevailed on to try his hand again at a species of his art which, well-versed operatic composer that he was, he probably thought himself but poorly equipped to explore with any chance of success. Many years had passed since his student days at Bologna under Sarti, who made him write innumerable *canti fermi* in the style of Palestrina, and he must have felt that the polyphonic facility thus acquired would not alone suffice for the creation of living works. Had it not been for an extraneous circumstance, it is doubtful whether anything would have induced him to approach once more, at the age of forty-eight, a style so widely different from that which he had but too exclusively pursued during the greater part of his past career.

The occasion which provided the impetus that was to unchain a whole series of church music was a request from the musical society at

Chimay, who sent a deputation to the castle to ask for a Mass for the approaching St. Cecilia's Day. The petition was received with Cherubini's habitual surliness, but his reluctance overcome, he settled down to write the Mass in F. Successful as the work proved, it was not until an official appointment brought him into closer contact with church music that Cherubini was led to discover, almost against his will at first, that he was capable of greater things in this domain of art. With the return of the Bourbons to the French throne, he came into royal favour, a blessing he had by no means enjoyed under Napoleon. Louis XVIII placed him at the head of the Chapel Royal in 1816, and he at once wrote a new Mass, the "Messe solennelle" in C, which was finished on March 14th of that year. To this succeeded the Requiem in C minor, composed at the end of 1816 for the anniversary of the death of Louis XVI. Three other Masses (E, G and B flat) followed before Cherubini's appointment as Director of the Paris Conservatoire in 1822, which once more drew his activities into new channels and gave him leisure for only two more important religious works, each occasioned by special circumstances. One of these is the Mass in A for the coronation of Charles X at Rheims on April 29th, 1825; the other the Requiem in D minor for male voices, written in 1836, to which a curious story is attached.

PORTRAIT OF CHERUBINI BY INGRES.

CHERUBINI IN CHURCH

Hiller* relates that Cherubini composed this Requiem for his own funeral, to save a repetition of the painful incident that had occurred at Bellini's death in 1834, when the priests of the Madeleine refused to admit female singers.

Although contemporary opinion and many later critics placed the second Requiem, written by a man of seventy-six, below the earlier and more ambitious Mass for the Dead, there can be no doubt to-day that it is immeasurably superior to all the rest of Cherubini's church music. It is the only one among these works that is still capable of making a profound impression, for alone among them it strikes an emotional note without forfeiting a truly ecclesiastical character. In spite of, or possibly because of, what in those days must have been modern audacity, it comes much nearer in spirit to the early polyphonic masters, and it was in connection with this work alone that Adolphe Adam† was justified in saying that "if Palestrina had lived in our own time, he would have been Cherubini." It is true that his youthful exercises *alla Palestrina* had a lasting effect upon his style and that none of his Masses in the least betray the practised hand of the opera composer, but then Cherubini's works for the stage are not truly dramatic and reveal the same cool detach-

* Article in Macmillan's Magazine, July, 1875.
† "Derniers Souvenirs d'un Musicien," 1859.

ment as his church music. Throughout his work he maintains the attitude of one who understands, but has little sympathy with, human joys and sufferings, just as in life he had neither justice nor benevolence to spare for his fellow musicians. If in Cherubini's church music we look for the intense human emotion of the B minor Mass or the *Missa Solennis*, we shall inevitably be repelled almost as if we had come into personal contact with his brusque and irritable nature. What has often been mistaken for grandeur in his work is rather the reflection of the gloom and acerbity that perpetually enwrapped a composer of whom a wit said he was the most even-tempered of mortals, for he was always ill-tempered. All the Masses are pervaded by a curious chill, from which only the second Requiem is almost entirely free—and it is characteristic of the composer's notorious egoism that it needed the thought of his own funeral to warm up his feelings. Although we are frequently—almost too frequently—struck by daring harmonic inventions, astonishing modulations and unexpected effects which give a momentary thrill; although we are surprised by the descriptive power, the dramatic turns, the exquisite writing for the voices, the stupendous contrapuntal architecture, we are left untouched, coolly admiring, at the end of it all. "Cherubini is like an extinct volcano, throwing out occasional flashes and sparks, but quite covered with cinders," said Mendelssohn, who, for all his great admiration of the composer, did not lose his head like most of his other contemporaries, two of whom called him "the last and noblest Roman in the purely classical style of art"* and "the most accomplished musician, if not the greatest genius, of the nineteenth century."†

To the musician of to-day the latter statement reads like an unintentional prophecy, for even to modern ears Cherubini's music is still full of genuine and frequently astonishing *accomplishment*, while it is now clearly seen to be devoid of true *genius*. The Masses are still worth studying and even deserve an occasional performance in the concert room, while the Requiem in D minor should certainly be no stranger to any male voice choir. Too impersonal to touch us deeply, these works are at any rate splendid pieces of decorative art. If they have neither sufficient human emotion nor melodic warmth to stir the hearer, they are on the other hand never tawdry, never theatrical, and they but very seldom recall the cheap tunefulness of the period, which has long made most of the composers of the same school unbearable. There is no frivolity about this music, which in its detached austerity is admirably ecclesiastical, even if in its lack of mysticism it suggests the atmosphere of a church

* Baillot.
† Oulibicheff.

where the penetrating cold light is unsoftened by stained glass and the imagination unaided by ceremony. But the absence of sentimentality is refreshing: such things as the frequent long *pianissimo* passages without any *crescendo* make a very agreeable impression of restraint, and the composer's fine sense of how to save up a climax is admirable. As a contrapuntist Cherubini need fear no rival, and Hiller is perfectly justified in saying that " the harmonies and modulations . . . seem actually and necessarily to proceed from the independent life of the separate parts, as they did with the old composers of the strict polyphonic style." There are moments approaching unqualified greatness in every work, but Cherubini's music is often spoilt by formal over-elaboration or repetition; the initial idea is nearly always striking, but its development is strained for the sake of symmetry. There is something exasperatingly neat and tidy, giving unwelcome glimpses of the man who had his handkerchiefs numbered consecutively, and even on his death-bed insisted on using them in the correct order.

In the Requiem and the Mass in D minor, the most perfect works among Cherubini's church music, it is difficult to trace any musical ideas of inferior value: everything is noble and lofty, and directly strikes the hearer's imagination, though not his feelings. The absence of a human note is compensated for by an equally conspicuous absence of the commonplace and the mundane. The other Masses are less consistently elevated and there are some movements, such as the Offertories in the Mass in C and the Coronation Mass that smack of the period and raise visions of the insipid melodiousness of Spontini or Donizetti.

If one has appraised Cherubini's Masses at their proper value and listens to them with commensurately modest expectations, they very seldom disappoint. They are neither great nor small enough to justify the amusing statement of Bellasis,* who speaks of " those four colossal Masses in D, the glory of the later church music, by Cherubini, Niedermeyer, Beethoven and Hummel " (!). Cherubini was a craftsman and, let it not be forgotten, a courageous innovator, who always looked out for something startling to say and invented many interesting effects. If they fall comparatively flat to-day, they are still capable of providing a certain amount of mild enjoyment, and incidentally they may have their use as a warning to those who are too readily captivated by novel combinations of sound without enquiring into the value of the ideas lying behind them. Cherubini shows that such effects are soon worn out if the breath of life be not in them.

* Edward Bellasis, Cherubini: Memorials Illustrative of his Life, 1874.

VIII. SMALL BEETHOVEN

VIII. SMALL BEETHOVEN

BEETHOVEN seldom accomplished anything supremely good in miniature. His songs and his small piano pieces clearly show that. He required elbow room, needed the space of extended forms in which to turn round. His short works lack that enormous vitality that animates his compositions on a larger scale. He more than any other master required the prop of the sonata form, which (as Wagner said) was the transparent veil through which he seemed to have looked at all music. The fact that he was so unsuccessful within small proportions is to be attributed to the peculiarity of his genius, which was constructive rather than inventive. His sketch books have shown clearly enough how toilsome a process the devising of his thematic material was, and it cannot be denied that even in its final form, considered separately, it is very frequently poor in quality. It is saved only, and gloriously saved, by the workmanship that ennobles it in the course of the development. The bricks Beethoven built with were square, rough and unattractive ; but, great architect that he was, he knew how to combine them into a magnificent edifice. In the hands of other composers, such things as the opening of the Finale of the "Kreutzer" Sonata might as well have grown into the most frivolous Italian overture, the principal theme of the "Eroica" into a harmless little minuet, instead of developing into towering movements.

Beethoven's manner of composition is like an avalanche. He begins with an insignificant clod of no particular force, and it is only when that lump of clay has been set rolling along the mountainous heights of his imagination that it gathers strength in accumulating other matter lying in its way, and so grows into an overwhelming power.

The works which show most clearly the lack of spontaneous and distinctive thematic invention in Beethoven are his short piano pieces. The songs are less reliable evidence, because they do not suffer from this defect alone, but also from that curious weakness that always seems to have beset Beethoven as soon as he attacked vocal music—a task for which he was constitutionally unfit. It is curious to note that the two longest among the small pieces give an undeniable support to the above observations. They are the best, and they interest us solely by reason of their evolution. In the "Andante Favori," originally intended as a slow movement for the "Waldstein" Sonata, the beautiful but rather nerveless tune is saved by the interesting peregrinations it makes through a curious blend of variation and rondo form, while the particularly uninspired theme of the Rondo a Capriccio ("The Rage over the Lost Penny") would be intolerable if it did not work its way through a wonderful, subtly graduated progression from petulant annoyance to raging fury. Beethoven becomes less interesting almost in exact proportion to the smaller number of bars in each piece. The two Rondos, Op. 51, merely conventionally developed, save for a wholly irrelevant episode in the Rondo in G, have a kind of pallid charm that soon wearies the hearer of the numerous repetitions of their rather vapid subjects. It was hardly a flattering tribute to the Countess Lichnowsky to dismiss an obligation by bestowing the second of these Rondos on her, while Giulietta Guicciardi, for whom it was originally intended, was given the Moonlight Sonata instead. But then, the dedication to the countess was an act of diplomacy, and that to Giulietta one of tender passion.

We next come upon the Fantasy (Op. 77), a curiously shapeless work, and utterly unlike Beethoven as regards working-out. There is, in fact, no structural development except a semblance of it in the final section. The piece begins in G minor, and rambles on through a number of keys, only to end in the remote tonality of B major. The slightly evolved last section has nothing whatever to do with what precedes it. The Fantasy can only be regarded as an experiment, more especially because it dates from approximately the same time as the equally indeterminate Choral Fantasy. Whatever it may have been that Beethoven tried to do, he wisely and hastily abandoned this free style, no doubt realizing that, desirable as it was, it could not express his particular individuality. But the Fantasy is interesting as an isolated example of what may well be taken as a specimen of his extempore playing. Had the gramophone existed in his time, a record of one of his improvisations at the piano would no doubt have preserved for us something very much like this piece.

A more firmly knit work is the Prelude in F minor, but this too is not representative of its composer, being a fairly successful emulation of Bach, whose unity of mood it certainly possesses. The other two Preludes (Op. 39), which modulate through all the major keys, departing from C major by way of the sharp keys, changing enharmonically at the end of the semicircle, and turning back over the flat keys, are quite uninspired ; but their curious form is not without interest. The first and longer Prelude is the better of the two, perhaps because it does not adhere as logically to the settled plan as the second. Instead of progressing rigidly, step by step, from one tonality to the next, as he does in the more closely-woven but very dry second Prelude, Beethoven here allows himself considerable freedom of modulation inside each fixed key. Thus, although defeating his object, he gives us better music, and the obvious conclusion is that the object cannot have been worth pursuing.

Two more small pieces, both belonging to the year 1810, are exceedingly barren. The Polonaise, dedicated to the Empress Elizabeth of Russia, shows all the signs of another obligation reluctantly performed, while the friendship that inspired the "Albumblatt für Elise" must have been a particularly placid and commonplace one. Nor is the little Rondo in A very exhilarating, but it has at any rate a certain innocent freshness that is mildly engaging.

The same amiable blandness characterizes several of the Bagatelles, Op. 33. They were written at different times between 1782 and 1802, and it is quite easy to lay one's finger on the early examples. They have a kind of good-natured gentleness that reminds one of demure Viennese citizens' wives and daughters in the coal-scuttle bonnets of the period. No. 2 might have been planned for the Scherzo of an early sonata ; but the caustic, almost fierce, humour of No. 7 is analogous in mood to the later movements in that form, and fits in more properly with the period of the eleven Bagatelles, Op. 119, to which the whimsical No. 6 also belongs. The later set again shows signs of having been written at different times. The first number was composed in 1822, Nos. 2 and 5 between 1800 and 1804, while the last five belong to the year 1820, when

Beethoven (like several other composers) was asked to contribute a few "trifles" to Starke's "Viennese Pianoforte School," a publication of which he can have thought but little. The curious fact is that the titbits he dashed off, no doubt hastily and with a bad grace, are among the best and most characteristic of his small pieces. The capricious motion of the sixth Bagatelle, the peculiar rhythmic climax of the seventh and the fine chromaticism of the eighth make little well-cut cameos of each of them. The most precious gem of the whole set, however, is the last, with its lovely melancholy repose.

But we must go to the third set of Bagatelles, Op. 126, if we wish to find the real Beethoven among his small works—and a Beethoven, too, we cannot discover quite like this anywhere else. For once, in the very last years of his life, he achieved a few masterpieces in miniature. He had at last learnt that his genius was capable of expressing itself even in condensed forms, and that true greatness need not necessarily resort to large proportions. It was his actual invention now, not his manner of developing, that was great and original. In the last Bagatelles, the whole personality of the man stands revealed to us. The first number is full of contemplative tenderness, not without an admixture of subtle irony. The second begins in ill-tempered commotion, gradually abating into a philosophical resignation ;

while the fourth, the longest of the set, is positively furious. The third piece is full of a pastoral grace, which has its counterpart in the fifth, each depicting, however, an entirely different landscape. The last piece is all placid rusticity between two little peevish outbursts at the beginning and the end. There are two more Bagatelles, without *opus* numbers, composed in 1797, and found among the sketches for the Sonata, Op. 10, No. 1. These are, again, in the early scherzo manner.

Beethoven's Bagatelles, as a whole, are certainly the only small piano works of his which can still give a considerable amount of pleasure to the modern musician. They are vastly divergent in style and extraordinarily unequal in quality ; but the playing of them is comparable to the joy of turning over a quaint collection of old-fashioned engravings of urban and rural scenes, interspersed with comic incidents sometimes in a bitterly malicious, sometimes in a grumpily indulgent vein, reminding us of certain scenes in Smollett or Sterne.

There are some still smaller piano pieces in the shape of Minuets, Ecossaises and Country Dances (*Ländrische Tänze*), which are quite negligible, although the last-named have a sort of fresh spontaneity that makes them look as if they had been sketched with much gusto during the master's walks in the environs of Vienna, perhaps at some wayside inn where a primitive rustic dance was in progress. And the Minuets here and there conceal the lion's claw under their smooth surface. They are the later *scherzi* in embryo.

In spite of the fact that some of the Bagatelles will remain a joy for all time, Beethoven's short pieces are unsatisfactory in the aggregate. He was decidedly a master of large forms only, and precisely because he is so great there, it is he more than anyone else who must be held responsible for the erroneous view that sublimeness in music is incompatible with a limited number of bars.

IX. THREE SPECIMENS OF EARLY MENDELSSOHN

IX. THREE SPECIMENS OF EARLY MENDELSSOHN

THE question why Mendelssohn began as a dazzling genius and ended as a mild talent presents a complex of psychological problems that cannot fail to interest the modern musician, however much he may be in sympathy with the prevailing fashion according to which it has become a thing of questionable taste to evince the slightest curiosity in this composer's work. If ever music had a favoured son, in the worldly sense, that son was Mendelssohn. Wealth, native wit, the most careful education, brilliant society and unbounded opportunities for experiment at home and experience abroad were his, in addition to natural gifts the easy flow and the precocity of which stand almost unrivalled in musical history. And yet how little did all this profit him in the long run; how quickly has the once brilliant lustre of his reputation become so badly tarnished that to-day a musical writer may scarcely venture to give it a shamefaced polishing-up without a more or less plausible apology. Mendelssohn, truly, was the spoilt child among composers, and it is not to be wondered at if the panegyrics that were showered on him by his contemporaries have made him almost insufferable to us who stand at a distance, and never came under the spell of his charming personality, which undoubtedly lent a fascination to his work it did not intrinsically possess.

But what exasperates us most in Mendelssohn is the fact that he never revolted against being thus hugged and petted. It is a deplorable thing indeed to witness how his music waxed increasingly wise and righteous as it grew up, how it became more and more genteel, and how its creator remained content with the conventions which are the discreet expedients of good form, thus dispensing with the necessity of shaping a more independent code of artistic manners likely to provoke bitter opposition from an age which demanded good form above all else. Mendelssohn had fire enough and to spare in his youth, but he saw no use in taking high leaps later in life, when he met with no obstacles. A boy may well jump high for sheer joy in his growing strength, but the mature man will be quite content to amble quietly along, and be thankful if no enemies present themselves.

Mendelssohn did take leaps in his youth. At a much earlier age, in fact, he sprang higher than any of the five musicians born within six years of him,* and had circumstances laid any difficulties in his path, there is little doubt that he would have striven to overcome them. But fate all too complacently traced out a smooth course for him, which he, worldly-wise but artistically

* Berlioz, Chopin, Schumann, Liszt and Wagner.

improvident, followed while others won for themselves a more lasting admiration by kicking over the traces and fighting strenuous battles. Life, handling them more severely, moulded them into stronger and more arresting personalities.

The child Mendelssohn is a character of an almost Barrie-like fantastic unreality, a Peter Pan turned upside down, who had never been anything but grown-up. At seventeen he was a master absolute, revealing not only a fully developed personality, but a perfection of technical realization verging on the incredible. Even before that insuperable youthful masterpiece, the "Midsummer Night's Dream" Overture, Mendelssohn had written works by no means negligible, such as the Octet, the first Symphony, Fugues and Symphonies for strings, and several little Operas, including "Die Hochzeit des Camacho."

The only three piano Sonatas of Mendelssohn's that were ever published* show in a very interesting manner the rapid development and the on-coming deterioration of this youthful genius, and they are so little known that we, in our modern detachment, may perhaps not altogether unprofitably bestow a glance upon them. The Sonata in G minor, published posthumously as Op. 105, was begun by Mendelssohn in June, 1820, at the age of eleven, but not finished until

* There are two MS. Sonatas at Berlin.

the August of the following year. During the intervening months the boy, whose father's wealth and hospitality easily brought him into touch with all the celebrities in and passing through Berlin, made the acquaintance of Weber, who visited the Prussian capital for the production of his "Freischütz." It is very curious to note the influence of the older master, who had by this time written his first three piano Sonatas, in the slow movement and finale of the boy's work, whereas in the first movement hardly a trace of it is to be found. Of Mendelssohn's own characteristic qualities there is little to be detected in the whole work, and what there is remains confined to the middle movement. The opening piece is pure Haydn, not only as regards thematic invention, but the peculiar manner of writing for the keyboard in a style that completely disregards a technique appropriate to the piano. The whole movement looks like the transcription of a string quartet, and even the most elementary pianistic devices prevalent at the time, such as the Alberti bass, are absent, a fact which on reflection argues a good deal of independence on the part of a child to whom such mannerisms must have been as familiar as his daily bread.

The first and last movements are strictly and stiffly classical, and the invention throughout is thematic, not melodic—that is to say, everything seems conceived, not spontaneously, but with a view to development. The principal subject of the first movement is worked out to a point of utter exhaustion, but it plays some clever and amusing pranks notwithstanding. The finale is a mixture of weak Haydn, pale Weber and bad Schubert, yet the easy grace of a perfectly rounded structure is already noticeable, for even when he talks the irresponsible nonsense of boyhood Mendelssohn never forgets to be perfectly well behaved. He belonged to that dreadful species of childhood which does not know how to be naughty.

In the Adagio, contrasting with the formality of the other movements, there is something of that mellow lyricism which in Mendelssohn's earliest works is still attractive, but soon ripens into a vague something made up of sentimentality, seemliness and somnolence that conjures up visions of the Victorian Sunday evening hour between tea and church. This slow movement, at any rate, is fresh and happy enough—a gracious tribute to Weber.

The Sonata in E major (Op. 6) was finished in March, 1826, shortly after Mendelssohn's seventeenth birthday, and a few months before the " Midsummer Night's Dream " Overture, which is as good as saying that the young musician had now reached full mastery over his manner and acquired astonishing originality of matter. The first movement is as characteristically and maturely

Mendelssohnian as anything he ever penned. He now writes natural melodies instead of pedantic themes, and his development has grown romantically free and poetical. In the working-out section, instead of twisting his material into aridly ingenious combinations, he lets it flow on unaffectedly, yet artfully, and frequently places it under new lights, like the figures of an epic that meet with various adventures. The little interrupting diminished-fifth figures in the bass, for instance, are miniature strokes of genius; so are the delightful accents on the weak beat in the Minuet, and the curious trumpet calls off the key in its Trio. Altogether this second movement is in Mendelssohn's best Scherzo manner.

The slow movement is an astonishing conceit if the composer's age and the period of the piece are considered. It is a kind of fugal recitative, the first half of which is written without time signature, a feature that has been hailed as an unheard-of innovation by some admirers of much more recent composers. Twice a short and rather mellifluous *andante* of nine bars intervenes, followed each time by an *allegretto* recalling the first movement, and thus presenting the germs of a cyclic form. This, on its second appearance, forms a bridge-passage conducting without a break into the finale, a spirited movement, where Mendelssohn, in his exuberance, loses his grip over his medium. What he now gives us is no longer piano music, but something like a brilliant orchestral overture not unskilfully transferred to the keyboard. There are fiery *tutti* effects intersected by charming little horn and flute episodes, and the swishing, flickering figures under which the second subject appears in the 'cello register are entirely violinistic. At the final climax Mendelssohn falls back into the manner of the Overture to "Camacho's Wedding" but he saves the situation in good time by once more recalling the first movement and thus rounding the work off quietly and imparting to it a feeling of poetical unity.

Taking the E major Sonata as a whole, it is difficult to find a more representative and attractive work in the whole of Mendelssohn's output. But the next year already saw a falling-off in his handling of the sonata form. In the Sonata in B flat major (posthumous, Op. 106), the ascendancy of sheer technical brilliance over imaginative quality, which was to go on increasing throughout his career, begins to make itself felt. From the point of view of sheer dexterity, the work is an advance on the E major Sonata, but it lacks the poetry and fanciful freedom of the latter. The first subject is again one of those themes laboriously devised to lend themselves to contrapuntal treatment, devoid of all imaginative impetus; and sure enough, it soon begins to coil itself into the most ingenious and meaningless patterns, imperfectly relieved by a second subject of a blandly insipid grace. The dear boy is now eighteen, and it is time to smooth down his rebellious locks with a little of that becoming macassar oil wherewith propriety demands to see the head of a perfect gentleman anointed. One has now had one's Overture performed at Stettin and one's Opera staged in Berlin, despite Spontini's intrigues ; one has visited Goethe, matriculated at the University with a metrical translation of Terence, and is attending Hegel's classes ; one proves rather good at Italian and landscape drawing, and at the grand musical parties at home one mixes freely with Heine, Holtei, Humboldt—to pick only one letter from a galaxy of celebrities ranging through the alphabet : in short, one had better become serious, even at the risk of being a little tedious. And so the third Sonata plods along tamely enough. There is indeed, in the Scherzo, a little of that fairy music Mendelssohn sometimes happily captured, but it is a fairy story told in a stuffy Berlin drawing-room full of dried bulrushes and paper fans. That there are also some oils in heavy gilt frames depicting moonlit peeps of the Rhine is made abundantly clear by the slow movement, which is charged with the sentiment of romantic German river legends. The finale, ushered in by an *allegro* reminiscent of the first movement—(who said the cyclic Sonata was invented by César Franck ?)—relapses for a moment into a rather insipid but not unattractive Weberian vein, but it proves so uneventful as it goes on that Mendelssohn, not unconscious of becoming dull, is compelled to recall his Scherzo half-way through the movement, which after some brilliant futilities trickles away very harmlessly.

From this point, Mendelssohn will go on for twenty years producing, with unfailing fluency, a mass of music often relieved by some piece or another delightful enough of its kind, but uniformly slick in an unenterprising sort of way, making his contemporaries rave over and posterity regret, nay resent, an accomplishment so great as to make one long for some hideous human aberration from its smooth path.

Mendelssohn's case is that of the very good boy who has got on everybody's nerves to such an extent that they wish to hear nothing more about him. Unhappily, the praises once so extravagantly showered on him make them disinclined to listen, had he something ever so charming to say. A pianist will sometimes take the risk of unearthing some particularly tedious old piece or producing some modern inanity, but the man who has the courage to revive even the best of the three Mendelssohn Sonatas, that in E major, is yet to be found.

X. THE MUSICAL DIARY OF LISZT'S TRAVELS

X. THE MUSICAL DIARY OF LISZT'S TRAVELS

ALTHOUGH no one doubts to-day that Liszt's reputation as a composer suffered unjustly from his fame as a virtuoso, the curse of his fabulous success as an interpreter is not yet wholly dispelled, and musicians remain reluctant to give him his due as the great constructive force in music he reveals himself to be to the careful and unprejudiced student. The blame, however, must be laid at his own door, for there is among his work—and more particularly among his piano music—as much chaff as there is wheat. Unhappily, too, the more worthless portion of it, eagerly seized upon by the few who were able to play it, and listened to with uncritical admiration by those who could not, is also the most obtrusive. Liszt was always a strange mixture of seer and showman, and the crowd will heed the showman while it passes by the seer unnoticed. It is none too surprising, therefore, that the piano pieces collected under the title of "Années de Pèlerinage" remained comparatively unknown to musicians at large, since they include, along with some indifferent and some inferior pieces, a number of magnificent works that reveal what John Payne has called the composer's "transcendent purity of aspiration and interstellar splendour of expression."

STEPCHILDREN OF MUSIC

Spanning as they do a period of several decades in Liszt's career, the " Années de Pèlerinage " constitute, apart from their musical value, an intensely interesting study of the evolution of his artistic outlook and of his gradual emancipation from a convention to which, it is true, he never stooped very low. The first set, containing impressions of Switzerland, was written during the Geneva period, in 1835-36 ; the second, dealing with Italian subjects, in Rome between 1838 and 1840 ; and the last at various places between 1862 and 1866. When the Swiss collection was first published in 1842, it was entitled " Album d'un voyageur," and comprised in three volumes a considerably larger choice of pieces. It has long been out of print, and many comparatively inferior numbers were eliminated from the composer's own revised edition.

Liszt, the father of the symphonic poem, a born programme musician, was at his best when a subject presented itself to him that happened to be in tune with his own peculiar musical expression. But he was seldom content with a mere adumbration of picturesque aspects ; he loved to go to the root of the matter and to intensify its underlying spirit in a way that was often full of poetic subtlety.

In the Swiss Album, which is entirely based on landscapes and aspects of nature, the prevalent moods are sublimated into a musical substance

Chapelle de Guillaume Tell

that seems to express, in analogous values raised on a higher plane, what the composer visualized. In "Au Lac de Wallenstadt" and "Au bord d'une source," the lazily lapping waters of the former and the rapid, gurgling spring of the latter, are etherealized into music of ineffable loveliness; nor is the very brilliant second piece in the least marred, as is too often the case with Liszt, by the exuberance of its texture, which in fact only enhances the harmonious sweetness, because it is so wonderfully adapted to the instrument. Three of the pieces in the same album are magnificent tone-pictures on a large scale. In the "Chapelle de Guillaume Tell" terrifying visions of the photochromes that one buys at Lucerne to make the memory of the rather cloying sweetness of that landscape a thing to be shunned, are happily banished by the human elements of a fine musical portrait of the national hero. "Orage," in spite of its stage thunder, and "Vallée d'Obermann," though it now and again threatens to lose its dignity through over-elaboration, are the two other great pieces in the volume. In the former there is some modern harmony that belongs to a much later period. It is the most difficult piece in the set, but again there is no suspicion of a mere piling-up of hair-raising technical feats for the sake of display; the work simply happens to be couched in such terms because the subject demands them. Liszt is, on the other hand, content with the utmost simplicity where he needs it, though never with shallow facility. The whole collection is thus distinguished by a perfect concord between intention and means of expression. The three simplest pieces in the Swiss book are the "Pastorale" with its rarefied Alpine atmosphere, the lovely "Eclogue" that has a sort of Virgilian purity, and "Le Mal du Pays," which explains the composer's being among the first to recognize Grieg's gifts of fixing down definite moods by means of short pieces. The least satisfactory number is the Nocturne, "Les Cloches de Genève"; its pretty tinkle becomes rather irritating, perhaps because it conveys only too well the somewhat complacent and somnolent character of the city of Calvin and Rousseau. The whole volume, it must be confessed, is not devoid of a suspicion of artificiality; the pictures of Switzerland are those of the cosmopolitan who is apt to be more immediately fascinated by a certain smug prettiness, and neglects to seek the rugged grandeur of the country.

The Italian set reveals a complete change of outlook. Here it is no longer nature that calls forth the best music in Liszt, but the Italian art and literature with which he saturated himself during his stay in Rome. There is about this volume a mellow glow that subdues even the moments of scorching passion and throws over them the soft, golden light of a southern sunset.

" Sposalizio," after Raphael's " Betrothal," is a glorious piece with all the fervent tenderness and limpid purity of its model, while " Il Penseroso," after Michelangelo's statue in the Mausoleum of the Medici at Florence, is so closely adapted to the subject in its contemplative seriousness that it scarcely satisfies as pure music. In " Sposalizio " there are once more some curious harbingers of later music : the opening phrase might be that of a Debussy Prelude, while the thirds and sixths and the diatonic contour suggest the only type of beauty worshipped by Strauss, an exclusive taste wherewith Liszt at any rate cannot be reproached. The three " Sonnets of Petrarch," originally written as songs, and only transcribed and elaborated in 1846, have all the nobility and aloofness of their texts, impaired here and there by an excessive saccharine admixture. They again show in a supreme measure Liszt's power of adapting his musical thought to the medium chosen for its expression : no vestige of song transcriptions clings to these superbly pianistic pieces, which draw an almost incredible wealth of wonderful sound effects from the instrument. The setting of a Canzonet by Salvator Rosa, though comparatively insignificant, comes like a refreshing morning breeze into the glamour of the other works in this book. The Fantasia quasi Sonata, " Après une lecture du Dante," is the most ambitious piece in the whole collection, and it is only the overwhelming greatness of the subject that makes it appear inadequate. There are in it, next to wonderfully impressive passages, some cheap ideas expensively decorated, and much of it is dazzling rather than truly stirring. A certain threadbareness of invention is frequently betrayed by the reiteration of similar figures through several keys, a trick too often resorted to by composers when inspiration runs to seed. But it is a magnificent piece for all its defects.

The supplement to the Italian set, "Venezia e Napoli," is only worth studying because it makes the "Années de Pèlerinage" representative of the whole of Liszt's pianistic inspiration by giving us some of the worst specimens of it. These three pieces—"Gondoliera," "Canzone" and "Tarantella"—are simply brilliant, showy and shallow transcriptions of some tawdry Venetian and Neapolitan airs, with an operatic tune by Rossini thrown in. Artistically they are negligible except for their masterly pianistic treatment.

The third volume is miscellaneous, both in style and in quality. For many reasons, more especially the numerous harmonic features that might belong to much later composers, this set is extremely interesting, but only three pieces in it are worth serious consideration as completely satisfactory music. They once again have their root in Italian soil : it is the Villa d'Este this time that has fascinated the master. The two Threnodies, "Aux Cyprès de la Villa d'Este," are intensely original and poignant, while "Les Jeux d'eau à la Villa d'Este" has a liquid, translucent brilliance that makes it, for all time, one of the finest musical suggestions of gushing waters, expressed not merely in generally musical but in specifically pianistic terms, a feature the work has in common with Ravel's "Jeux d'eau." The "Angelus (Prière aux Anges Gardiens)," originally composed for string quartet, is a piece of unrelieved dullness that only arouses a mild interest by reason of its harmony, which makes one think of César Franck. But it is Franck at his worst, when he evokes visions of brightly coloured plaster saints. The other "religious" piece in the book, a "Sursum corda," is like a bad mixture of incense and cheap scent. The two remaining works, "Sunt lacrymæ rerum" (in Hungarian style), and the "Funeral March" for the Emperor Maximilian I of Mexico, are curiously fantastic and shapeless pieces that leave a vague sense of something very daring and original left unaccomplished.

Liszt, with the prophetic sympathy he never failed to extend to the most audacious experiments of the worthiest among his younger contemporaries, sometimes appears himself to have endeavoured to step so far into the unknown that he was inevitably doomed to lose himself and fail. But it is precisely this love of exploration that often makes his failures more interesting and valuable than his successes.

XI. WAGNER'S FRENCH SONGS

XI. WAGNER'S FRENCH SONGS

IN the summer of 1839, Wagner, accompanied by his diminutive first wife and his enormous Newfoundland dog, descended on Paris, fully expecting, in the flush of his twenty-six years, to take the French capital by storm. But his self-confidence, highly developed as it already was at that time, was soon to receive more than one rude check. Nothing succeeded with him. He was at once too immature and too profound for the Parisians of the period. Meyerbeer's patronage gained him nothing more than a courteous but unprofitable reception from the mighty of the musical world ; and in some quarters, indeed, it was not regarded as too high a recommendation. Heine, for one, declared that it made him suspicious of the young man. It is certainly not inconsistent with all we know of Meyerbeer's character to take it for granted that he would have hesitated to take Wagner under his wing, had he thought it likely that he would be outstripped by him one day.

The sketches of "Rienzi" met with a good deal of cool politeness at the opera, and, being the work of a young foreigner who had nothing but his earnest striving after an as yet unattainable ideal to speak in his favour, they were dismissed with a benevolent word of encouragement. The "Faust" Overture, begun late in 1839, after a rehearsal of Beethoven's Ninth Symphony at the Conservatoire, a work far superior to "Rienzi," met with a proportionately greater lack of understanding. Liszt, that fairy godfather of all young musicians of genius, adored just then by all Paris, was so cordially disliked by the jealous Wagner that the first meeting failed to lead to an intercourse which could not have been but of the greatest benefit to him.

There was nothing for it but to pander to popular taste. Wagner's friends, Lehrs and Anders, advised him to write some small songs, to be offered to eminent singers for performance, and they undertook to ransack French poetry for suitable words. Wagner managed to get a set of "Trois Mélodies" published in 1840, but the great vocalists held back. Pauline Viardot, to whom Wagner was anxious to introduce them first, was appreciative, but with more discernment than kindness, saw no reason why the songs should be brought before the public, at any rate by her; Dumont, third tenor at the opera, objected to the words as not being fashionable; Gérardy, a very popular concert singer, was ready with another excuse; and so all along the line. The songs did little to stem the tide of misery which engulfed the unfortunate musician and his wife; they barely sufficed to hold starvation at bay. Things grew even worse when Wagner, having moved into better quarters in anticipation of the production of some translated portions of " Das Liebesverbot" at the Théatre de la Renaissance, heard that this work was withdrawn on account of the establishment's failure. A vaudeville, " La Descente de la Courtille," which he had composed, fared a little better, for, although it was rejected because the chorus declared it to be unsingable, one song at least was retained and had an ephemeral success. For the rest, a most precarious livelihood had to be eked out by arrangements of pianoforte scores of operas, transcriptions of favourite airs as cornet solos, and the like.

The first French poem that Wagner set to music in the hope of making his fortune was a lullaby which Anders had obtained from a poetically-inclined friend of his. The world has no cause to regret that the name of its author has not been preserved ; it is nothing more than a conventional, tenderly sorrowful ditty of a widowed mother over her sleeping baby. The music has a captivating charm mixed with a certain monotony which made Minna Wagner exclaim with unconscious penetration, when the composer tried it over late one night, that it was " a lovely thing to send one to sleep." Of personality the song has scarcely a trace, although, needless to say, ingenious commentators have not failed to find in it, on the ground of very slight external resemblances, a close relationship to the Spinning Song in " The Flying Dutchman."

One Bruno Sauer, in fact, provided a German version which makes both a spinning song and a lullaby of it, alluding, not without grace, to the still dormant song of Senta by making the mother look forward to the day when life shall begin for her child, whose beauty shall then become manifest to the world.

The setting of Ronsard's "Mignonne" is no less attractive and no more original. It is just the pretty French romance of the period, no better and no worse than a hundred others. But that very fact, perhaps, makes it remarkable, for it is certainly curious that one of the most German of composers should have adapted himself with such complete ease to a style that was utterly foreign to his temperament, and that he should have handled so perfectly a language for which he had no liking.

The least commonplace of the "Trois Mélodies" is "Attente," from Victor Hugo's "Orientales," but its originality is gained by a sacrifice of elegance. Wagner wrote badly for the piano. He must have thought orchestrally from the beginning, and, indeed, the repeated staccato chords of this song would have made a delightful accompaniment for wood-wind and horns, such as we frequently come across in his music-dramas; but on the piano it is almost unbearable. Glasenapp sees in "Attente" a presage of passages in "Tristan," as if a mere thematic resemblance meant anything.

Another song dating from 1840 is "Tout n'est qu'images fugitives," on a very insignificant poem by Jean Reboul, the most interesting portion of the manuscript of which is its cover, since it bears the first sketch of the "Faust" Overture. What it encloses is of little importance, save for the fact that a strong tendency towards a descriptive-dramatic style is already very apparent. It is, however, entirely out of place in a song that should be purely lyrical. The attempt at depicting a real storm at the comparison of man to a "navigator of a tempestuous day," cleverly as it is realized, places the whole song on a wrong plane. The melody is as trivial as the words, but the contrast between the earthly and the celestial elements is drawn with a certain amount of nicety, and the accompaniment is not too unpianistic for once.

A very curious work for Wagner is "Les Adieux de Marie Stuart" to words by Béranger, written on March 26th, 1840. This again has an indisputably French *allure* ; it is not the work of a masquerading German. Of true dramatic feeling there is not an atom. Be it said that Mary's farewell to France, her adopted country, merely masks a sentimental patriotic effusion on the part of the poet, which the young composer who felt himself so shabbily treated by the French capital could hardly be expected to take seriously ; but when the unhappy queen warbles glib cadences to the words "To leave thee is to die," it is hard to believe that this can be Wagner, even at his worst. Meyerbeer is rampant here; and there is more than a suspicion that Wagner took a few hints how to please the public from Halévy, some of whose operas he was then engaged in arranging for the piano. The whole song has all the shallow pomp of "Rienzi," and that opera is in fact indebted to it for a passage in Adriano's monologue in the third act.

One more French song remains to be dealt with: the most curious of all. On December 29th, 1840, Wagner wrote to Schumann: "I hear that you have composed Heine's 'Two Grenadiers,' and that at the end occurs the 'Marseillaise.' I, too, have set it to music last winter and have also used the 'Marseillaise' at the finish. That means something! My 'Two Grenadiers' is written to a French translation which I got made here and which Heine found satisfactory." It means something indeed that two great composers, each without knowledge of the other's doing so, should have hit on the grotesque idea of making two Napoleonic soldiers express their ardent devotion to the Emperor to the strains of the most republican of songs. The anxiety with which Wagner sought to convince Schumann that the notion had occurred to him first more than half reveals his smouldering annoyance at having thus collided with a composer

WAGNER (AETAT 29) DRAWING BY KIETZ.

whom he was the more ready to disparage because he was just then palpably indebted to him for more than one passage in the very Schumannesque "Faust" Overture. For several reasons Wagner's setting of "The Two Grenadiers" proved less popular than Schumann's, although the latter is as much overrated as the former is undervalued and the two meet half-way in a touching union of mediocrity. To begin with, Schumann's version is more melodic and superficially pleasing. Next, there may have been some sound sense in Gérardy's objection to Wagner's work, already hinted at, that, as far as Paris was concerned, the use of the Marseillaise could not be a popular device just then, since the song was to be heard only to the accompaniment of guns and fighting in the streets. Then again, although Wagner's song has some fine dramatic moments and, as a German critic has justly pointed out, the Marseillaise is far more impressive through being kept to the accompaniment only instead of being drawn into the voice as in Schumann's setting, it must be confessed that once again the song is marred by the miserable style of its pianistic writing. But the greatest disadvantage of all lies in the fact that the French version by Loeve-Veimars so distorts the rhythm of Heine's poem that the original text cannot possibly be fitted to Wagner's music. There are only three things to be done : "The Two Grenadiers" must either be sung in French, or it must be sung translated into a different German version, or it must not be sung at all. The last expedient, all considered, seems the most advisable : except for an occasional dusting and exhibiting as a curiosity, " The Two Grenadiers," like the rest of Wagner's French songs, may well be left resting in peace in the lumber-room of musical history.

XII. A GERMAN PRECURSOR OF SULLIVAN

XII. A GERMAN PRECURSOR OF SULLIVAN

JUST as England had her one composer of light opera in the second half of the last century, so Germany possessed a solitary and somewhat similar figure during its first half in the person of Albert Lortzing. He stands alone as a purely German representative of the *genre*, for Offenbach must be attributed to the French school of comic opera, and Flotow, the other possible rival, is at least partly French by training. The Viennese operetta, on the other hand, is so entirely a home product of the Austrian capital that it is connected with Germany by nothing but its language.

Lortzing is over-rated in his own country and unduly neglected everywhere else. It may be held that his music is too flimsy and commonplace to be worth exporting, and that even the student of musical history can well afford to ignore a minor German composer who has done nothing sufficiently strong to perpetuate his particular style. Both arguments, however, are only relatively valid. It cannot be denied that Lortzing's music, regarded as music pure and simple, is worth little ; but in comparison with the sorry stuff that is served up under the name of musical comedy to-day, any of the two or three of his best works would prove a healthy, graceful and musically charming entertainment, even if we disregard the fact that his libretti are neatly constructed and full of good points. And the fact that Lortzing created no school does not place him beneath the historian's notice. Is there no interest in studying a personality, even a comparatively unimportant one, who stands alone as a representative of a distinctive style at a particular period of a country's musical career? While in Paris and Vienna the operetta flourished and enchanted the public by its effervescent charms, in Germany Lortzing was left alone to give a more sedate public a similar kind of enjoyment, clumsier in wit and more sober in style, but nevertheless productive of laughter and heart-easing diversion. His is a kindly, sunny humour, for he never ruffled his placid audiences by any too cruel thrusts of satire. It has, in fact, a great deal of the sentimentality of the old German *Singspiel*, a quality which often characterizes and sometimes disfigures his music. The comic portions of his operas always have a lively aptness, enhanced by his happy knack of neat orchestration; but where it is a question of displaying tender or melancholy feelings, he lapses sadly into an almost unendurable triviality. Most of his operas contain a few songs of this kind, which even to-day retain the popularity of folk-songs in Germany. The reason for this is not far to seek, for these songs have the same artless simplicity, bordering on inanity, and the same amount of maudlin *Gemüt*, which make so much of German folk-music unacceptable to other nations.

Lortzing's life was one long, pathetic struggle against poverty and the consequences of an incomplete education. He was born in Berlin on October 23rd, 1803. His father, an actor who perpetually wandered from town to town, could not give him any opportunities for regular study, but the boy showed remarkable natural aptitude, and at the age of nine could play the piano, the violin and the violoncello. He appeared frequently both as singer and actor, in whatever juvenile parts were going at the theatre at which his father happened to be engaged, acquiring almost automatically an extraordinary facility in contriving effective stage situations. Being thus saved the trouble of finding a librettist, he was able to write the words and music of his first Opera, "Ali Pascha von Janina," at the age of twenty-one. Settled down at Cologne, where he had married in 1823, he continued for several years the humdrum life of a provincial actor and opera singer, gaining still greater stage experience the while. The only work of importance he wrote during this period was, curiously enough, an Oratorio on the subject of the Ascension, a task for which he was temperamentally unfit and technically ill-equipped. In 1833, at last came an engagement from Leipzig, where he passed the only relatively happy ten years of his life as first tenor. Two

Operas were produced in 1837: the now almost forgotten "Die beiden Schützen" (The Two Riflemen) and the still popular "Zar und Zimmermann" (Tsar and Carpenter)*, the latter of which was at once performed all over Germany. A few works that followed fell flat, but in 1842 came "Der Wildschütz" (The Poacher), for which he had very ingeniously turned a flippant but amusing comedy of Kotzebue's into a capital libretto. So great was the success of this Opera that Lortzing now decided to give up acting. Two years later, the Leipzig Theatre appointed him to the post of conductor, but this engagement by no means proved an auspicious event. Lortzing's kindly nature exposed him to the caprices of singers and orchestra, and his defective training made it still harder for him to maintain his authority. Disheartened and embittered, he resigned his conductorship in 1845, and the success of "Undine," produced at Hamburg and Leipzig that year, did not fully compensate him for his disappointment. 1846 found him in Vienna for a short time as conductor to the historical "Theater an der Wien," where he produced "Der Waffenschmied" (The Armourer). But once again, to his distress, he found himself unable to hold his position with dignity, and from that moment began a very precarious existence. He was obliged to travel

* Known in England under the title of "Peter the Shipwright."

about with a numerous family, earning an uncertain livelihood by acting and conducting his own operas. His success was waning, and all the important theatres rejected his later works, which bore traces of the exhaustion of that care-free charm and high spirits which had carried his earlier comedies over the footlights. In 1850 a Berlin theatre offered him a pittance for conducting farces and vaudevilles, and on January 21st, 1851, he died in his native city, completely worn out by worry and neglect. It was only then that the public remembered the many joyous hours he had given them, and his tragedy ended with the crowning irony of a pompous funeral.

Like Sullivan, Lortzing was completely successful in no domain of music but that of comic opera, but this similarity of results was produced by entirely different causes. In the case of the German composer we feel that it was sheer inability that precluded him from rising above the expression of lighthearted flippancy or mawkish sentimentality ; the Englishman, on the other hand, has proved that he was capable of dealing with more elevated subjects, but his Savoy successes amounted to such a fashionable craze that he had to thrust all other efforts into the background in order to satisfy a rapacious public with new entertainment. The comic opera style of both composers is light, but Lortzing's music is so because he could not help it, whereas in Sullivan we are conscious of deliberately restrained resources with an immense reserve of strength and workmanship behind them. Sullivan's art is accomplished fluency, Lortzing's agreeable garrulity. The former's music, even when made of slender material, has substance; the latter's is nothing more than an attractive drapery thrown over an unsteady scaffolding. Over both presides the spirit of genuine comedy, and both fail when they attempt serious opera. But here again they fail in different ways. A great deal of Sullivan's "Ivanhoe" is much too good to have deserved the cruel fate with which it met on the unhappy opening of the Royal English Opera House in Cambridge Circus; much of Lortzing's "Undine" is not nearly good enough to justify the popularity the work still enjoys in its native country after more than three quarters of a century.

It is a curious fact that composers with a real gift for comedy are the ones who lapse most grievously into false sentiment when they attempt to become serious. A comic musician, when he becomes sentimental, is capable of the most maudlin perpetrations known in his art. Tchaikovsky, soon after the amusing "Nutcracker Ballet," vented a neurotic grief in the "Pathetic Symphony," Sullivan wrote mawkish church music between his most high-spirited comedies, Chabrier composed a masterpiece of lachrymation in "Gwendoline," and Offenbach infused much unendurable insipidity into the "Tales of Hoffmann." Literary humorists, by the way, are by no means exempt from this curious complex : Dickens, Mark Twain, George du Maurier, Alphonse Daudet and many others suffer from it. Lortzing, like Offenbach, was ill at ease with a fantastic subject, and his "romantic fairy opera" ("Undine") is good only in the few numbers that afford comic relief. All the rest, but for isolated flashes of true inspiration, is shabbily worked. There are glimpses of the influence of Weber, especially in the slight use of the *Leitmotiv*, and of Marschner, but they are due to nothing more than the experienced opera-singer's rough and ready familiarity with these composers' devices, which he resorts to with but too much freedom. A watered-down Mendelssohnian idiom, too, is discernible in "Undine," and from the whole of Lortzing's work it is evident that he knows and loves Mozart. But, although he has the greatest master of comedy in music always at the back of his mind, he is unable to make any really profitable use of this consciousness. Nevertheless, a certain facility in dishing up other composers' tricks in an attractive form, sufficiently disguised or enfeebled to deceive the ordinary listener, stood him in good stead. He seems to have gone through life like Cadwallader Crabtree, pretending to be deaf in order to catch other people's secrets. He lacks authority as composer as he did as conductor; at tense dramatic moments, all his strength of character and all his learning, such as they are, forsake him, and he carries off timidly situations that require the vigorous, sweeping handling of genius. And, being without audacity, he has scarcely any originality—a defect that is most glaringly apparent from his endings, which are almost invariably cut to one or other of the few commonplace patterns of the period. In the manner in which he concludes a piece, more than in anything else, a composer shows how much individuality he possesses. It is enough to compare Bach's infinitely varied endings with the stereotyped closes of Handel to make one marvel that the former's vast superiority over the latter could ever have been questioned.

In Lortzing's comic operas, however, the slender texture of his music is not very detrimental to its effect; and it is, moreover, compensated for by his delightfully transparent and piquant orchestration, which gives it enough surface attractiveness to bring it off effectively. Of the four works which are still in the repertory of every German opera house, "Undine" would be doomed to certain failure, and the too sentimental "Tsar and Carpenter" to an indifferent reception in any other country. But "The Poacher" and "The Armourer" might well be revived by some of our excellent amateur operatic societies ; and if one day somebody would give us the longed-for "London Opéra Comique," which should do all that the Paris house no longer does, these two works would have to be included in the repertory as representative of the only purely German composer of comic opera of the early nineteenth century.

XIII. A VICTIM OF HIS POPULARITY

XIII. A VICTIM OF HIS POPULARITY

THERE is scarcely a figure in the whole history of music that has been painted to posterity in more unpleasant hues than that of the Russian composer Alexander Nicolaevich Serov. Has ever musician made himself more unbearable to his fellow artists than he contrived to do by his sycophancy, his arrogance, and by the mixture of ready compliance and overweening conceit that so magnetically attracted the multidude ? Serov has long been overtaken by the contemptuous neglect with which the public never fails, sooner or later, to treat an artist who has cheated it of its real spiritual needs by dazzling it for a time with glitter and shallow sensation ; and his punishment is the greater precisely because his blandishments were so completely successful in their time. The puppets of his making, which once thronged the Russian operatic stage, insolently barring the way to the truly human figures created by Moussorgsky, Borodin and Rimsky-Korsakov, have no longer even a semblance of life, now that no one troubles to pull the wires Serov himself handled with such consummate skill.

Little is to be gained, perhaps, by a critical examination of Serov's three operas ; yet it is never entirely unprofitable to look at the work of a man whose transient glory has irretrievably vanished, and to speculate on the reasons of his success and the causes of his eventual downfall. As works of art, these operas are wholly negligible, but as documents relating to the curious history of Russian opera and the triumph of its national ideals, they will always retain some little interest. Besides, Serov himself, unsympathetic as he must be to all who judge him by the evidence of his contemporaries, is not without a certain attractiveness. He compels the kind of involuntary admiration we grant to sound acting of the villain's part in a third-rate melodrama. It is impossible to help paying a reluctant tribute to a man who, holding an obscure official post in a little provinical town, took corresponding lessons in counterpoint from a professor living a thousand miles away, who fought with a smouldering resentment against his technical weakness and creative dullness and who, later on, at over forty years of age and after having made himself universally detested for his musical criticism, grimly resolved to overcome all these shortcomings and difficulties by obstinately ignoring their existence.

Serov was born at St. Petersburg in 1820. He was given an excellent education and pursued legal studies, making at that time the acquaintance of Vladimir Stassov, to whom he was at first linked in a friendship that was not destined to withstand the radical difference of artistic views which arose later between these two critics. For a critic's career it was that Serov embraced in 1850, when he had succeeded in freeing himself from his government appointment. Until the age of forty, he studied music and composed in a desultory manner, always passionately desiring to enforce his doctrines by a compelling example of his own, yet never free from doubt as to his own powers of embodying artistic views that were. after all, of an almost entirely destructive order, An operatic version of "The Merry Wives of Windsor," attempted in 1843, ran to seed. As a critic, he was violent, hasty and indeterminate, and, as Mrs. Rosa Newmarch tells us in her clear-sighted study of Serov,* there is no trace of any well-ordered critical philosophy to be found in his writings. According to a statement of his own, his likes and dislikes were characteristically miscellaneous. He admired Beethoven and Weber, liked Mendelssohn, and worshipped Meyerbeer. Chopin he loved, while Schumann and "all his disciples" (whoever they may be) repelled him. He had a taste for Liszt, with many reservations, and adored Wagner, whose later works he considered as the outcome of Beethoven's symphonic style. In 1858 he went to Germany and returned more completely under the sway of Wagner than ever.

At length, under the influence of such divergent

* Rosa Newmarch: "The Russian Opera." (Herbert Jenkins.)

views, and exasperated by the isolation he had created for himself as a critic, he set about the composition of " Judith " on a libretto by K. I. Zvantsiev, based on Giustiniani's drama, " Giuditta." The librettist, who was the first Russian translator of Wagner, began to doubt Serov's capability to bring the work to a successful issue ; he abandoned the book, which was completed by D. Lobanov. Serov's setting was finished early in 1862, and already in May of that year the first performance took place in St. Petersburg, Serov having won an influential patron in the Grand Duchess Helena Pavlovna, an exalted protectress of music with more enthusiasm then discernment.* The splendour with which the work was mounted and the superficial brilliance of its music gained it an extraordinary success. Serov, who was still haunted by doubts during the process of composition, must himself have been not a little astonished at this result ; but it was not in his nature to betray signs of grateful surprise, and he proved only too ready to accept the public verdict and believe the work to be a masterpiece. Wagner on his visit to Russia in 1863, completed the turning of his head by praising the orchestration of " Judith." Serov did not suspect his idol, as there was but too much reason to do, of singling

* Moussorgsky caricatured both Serov and the Grand Duchess in his burlesque song, " The Musician's Peep-Show."

out this one commendable feature because it was advisable to pay as flattering a compliment as possible to a composer whose unreserved adulation demanded an attitude at once polite and politic.

It has sometimes been taken for granted that Wagner's hold on Serov implied a dominating influence on the latter's work ; a perusal of the vocal scores of Serov's three operas shows, however, that there is very little of Wagnerian matter, or even manner, to be discovered there. Were the full scores accessible, it would probably be found that whatever influence there may be is entirely confined to the instrumentation. Stassov, in fact, shrewdly hints at such a state of affairs when he declares that although Serov was a fanatical admirer of Meyerbeer, he yet seized the *superficial* characteristics of Wagner. But admiration of Meyerbeer and of Wagner is by no means incompatible, for the surface elements in the latter do actually emanate from the former, as may not only be plainly seen in " Rienzi," but still sufficiently clearly in many a passage in the later works.

Serov's operas are wholly lacking in form and style. They are a succession of separate, often fragmentary and shapeless, musical movements, strung together by recitatives as dry as any *recitativo secco*, although fully and at times pompously accompanied. A hearing of one of the operas must be like a tedious walk through a number of dull, tortuous alleys leading from one more or less uninteresting point to another, with occasional halts at some edifice that is not without a showy exterior, but devoid of anything arresting within. "Judith," the most factitious of the three works, was also the most successful, because its libretto gave Serov plenty of opportunity for a display of his undeniable talent for colouring up situations of mere external scenic lustre. Like Meyerbeer, he is at his best when dealing with glittering processionals and sumptuous ballets: the March and the Dances in "Judith" are, in fact, quite good show-pieces. Of psychology or genuine pathos, however, there is no vestige. Serov was not interested in any aspects of his texts but those which directly strike the spectator; that it is the mission of music to voice the most intimate emotions of the characters, he seems not even to have suspected. In tense situations he is perfectly content with the most worn-out devices: the tremolo, the sentimental 'cello tune, the fussy agitation of a stretto, and that worst of all dramatic tags, the chord of the diminished seventh—such are the tricks which we must invariably expect with certainty at a dramatic crisis. Never by any chance has the composer a surprise in store for us, never do we get even a hint of a personal note or a thought the like of which we have not heard a hundred times before.

Yet, time was when all this was gratefully

lapped up by the public, and it mattered little to Serov that it was the wrong kind of public who idolized him. So long as it represented the majority, he thought he could afford to ignore the few people who foresaw the blow which the new, living and racy art of a Moussorgsky and a Borodin would soon deal to his paste-board creations.

But now Serov made the mistake of his life, the one mistake which even the most adoring followers among the masses never forgive—he improved. In the autumn of 1865, his second opera, "Rogneda," was ready for production. The subject, this time, was a Russian one, dealing with the early conflicts of Paganism and Christianity. The libretto gave less scope for broad scenic effects and imperiously demanded at least an attempt at national colour. Almost insensibly the man who posed as a bitter opponent of the rapidly growing national school, took a few leaves out of its book. With unfailing instinct, of course, he seized only the most superficial features of his country's folk-song, which he polished and smoothed down to suit his own shallow personality; but even this was too daring an enterprise for a section of the public that worshipped usage, and its attitude towards the composer began to cool. Having grown a little taller, he thought it safe to shorten the stilts he had been walking on ; his gait thus became rather more natural, but he was now less conspicuous to the crowd.

Serov was not to see the final falling-off of his hold on opera-goers at large. It was well for a nature like his, which would scarcely have found compensation in the greater sympathy with which his third opera was looked upon by his more advanced contemporaries. "The Power of Evil," based on a play by Ostrovsky, begun in 1867, and left incompletely scored on Serov's death in 1871, contains some popular scenes which have unmistakably grown on Russian soil. They make one feel that, had Serov not persisted with a false pride in his antagonism, he might have become a valuable asset to the national movement. But he still remained as incapable as ever of drawing living individual figures, and his invention was still poor, his harmony monotonous and his rhythm flat and dull. Nevertheless, there is a feeling of greater humanity, because the whole work is on a smaller scale ; it has no longer the inflated appearance of the music in the earlier works, but is more proportioned to the composer's own littleness.

Thus, even before his end had come, Serov had begun to present a melancholy example to the world ; through him it was made plain that an artist who has once won the affection of the largest and shallowest public cannot, for the rest of his life, afford to aim higher. If he does, he will only be deserted by that public without being accepted by people of artistic culture.

XIV. THE EARLY TCHAIKOVSKY SYMPHONIES

XIV. THE EARLY TCHAIKOVSKY SYMPHONIES

THE frequent appearances of the fourth, fifth and sixth of Tchaikovsky's Symphonies on concert programmes does not seem to awaken any curiosity in the concert-goer as to the earlier three. It is rather complacently taken for granted that the later works, being so regularly performed, must be infinitely superior to those which are so persistently neglected. But it would be as well to remember that what is thrown into the balance and found wanting is often but very slightly less weighty than that which is accepted as genuine value. There is, in fact, no vast difference between the quality of the earlier and the later triad of Tchaikovsky's Symphonies.

The first Symphony (Op. 13, in G minor), which bears the sub-title of "Winter Day-Dreams," was composed in 1866, when Tchaikovsky was twenty-six years of age. The work gave him infinite trouble, and was the direct cause of the insomnia and nervousness he suffered from at the time, which, aggravated by his consciousness of technical inexperience, eventually led to a terrible nervous breakdown that verged dangerously on madness.

Yet he worked at it day and night in a kind of obsession. When he at last submitted the Symphony to his former masters, Anton Rubinstein and Zaremba, in the hope that they might give it a hearing at one of the Musical Society's concerts, both severely critized and rejected it. In February, 1867, the two middle movements were at last performed in St. Petersburg, with very scant success, but a better reception was accorded to the whole work a year later. The Symphony was then laid aside until 1883, when the Moscow Musical Society revived it.

The first movement, "Winter Dream on the Road," is the best, an attractive study in grey, conjuring up visions of a *troïka* gliding swiftly over a snowy plain under a leaden sky. The melancholy thoughts awakened by the desolate landscape are almost painfully real, and the whole piece has that definiteness of mood and that unity of construction which often make even the longest of Tchaikovsky's movements appear as if they were the result of one single thought. After that the work falls off. The slow movement, "Dreary land, land of mists," fully justifies the adjective in its title. It begins with a good, though sentimental, theme which afterwards recurs *ad nauseam*, smothered in a welter of meaningless embroidery which, instead of propping it up, only makes it appear the more spineless. A second melody, far from providing relief, still intensifies this cloying mawkishness. Long before the main theme bursts forth hysterically, enwrapped in melodramatic tremolos, it has become exasperatingly wearisome, and when at last it dies out exhausted, as well it may, we only too gladly turn to the *Scherzo*. This—at any rate its principal section—is graceful and innocently amusing in the ingenious way in which a single rhythmic figure is exploited without too much monotony. But the *Trio* is the worst part of the whole Symphony, a cheap, tawdry waltz tune suggestive of a ballroom crowded with insipid ladies clad in the fashion of the period, a transition from the crinoline to the bustle. When the *Scherzo* has been heard over again, its persistent rhythm is cleverly combined with the theme of the *Trio* in a charming little *coda*. The *Finale* begins very promisingly with a lugubrious slow introduction that is adroitly built upon a short phrase, but the ensuing *allegro* is uncompromisingly dull. The first subject is one of those themes which, utterly devoid of character, lend themselves very easily to contrapuntal development. Tchaikovsky forthwith falls into the snare from which, though he feels far from comfortable in it, he is unable to extricate himself. There is no true contrapuntal workmanship, although the theme is turned and twisted about and appears continually in some modified form or another ; it never blossoms out into new ideas, but goes on repeating the same message to the end. The varied passage-work by which it is surrounded never assumes any significance ; it is so much padding, the dry wood shavings that enwrap the cheap ware and save it from breakage without doing anything to enhance its value. The second subject is no more than a superficially attractive melody decked out in tinsel. After a good deal of clumsy *fugato*, the return of the opening *andante* brings an impressive moment of definite feeling, a tangible mood-picture, into all this shallow jangling. If the work only ended on this note it would have a certain unity of atmosphere, but Tchaikovsky must needs build up a huge peroration in which he vouchsafes nothing more than the repeated information that he is about to finish, which he eventually does in the most pretentiously grandiloquent manner.

The second Symphony (Op. 17, in C minor) is unique among the six, for it shows most conspicuously a national influence from which, on the whole, Tchaikovsky held aloof. It was written in 1872, at a time when he was in somewhat close contact with the "Invincible Band" in St. Petersburg, and it is based on Little-Russian themes. But it is not national for this reason alone, for the mere use of Russian songs does not necessarily make Russian music, as Tchaikovsky has abundantly proved elsewhere ; it is mainly the *treatment* of the theme that makes this music autochthonal in the sense advocated by Balakirev. Its freshness, its bright colours and the open-air feeling it reveals, for once show us the composer as a healthy child of nature, who refrains from making every impression he receives an excuse for insisting on his real or imaginary troubles. The "Invincibles" were delighted with the Symphony, except Cui, who expressed himself very scathingly about a work that went a long way towards fulfilling the ideal which he himself continually preached, but so imperfectly practised. Seven years later Tchaikovsky himself pronounced the work to be immature and mediocre, and he undertook a complete revision, leaving only the *Finale* intact.

The first movement has a slow introduction based on a melancholy folk-song, and the *allegro* is built on two delightful and well-contrasted subjects, which are developed with much greater resourcefulness than anything in the preceding Symphony. Moreover, the music nowhere deteriorates into mere lifeless patterns, and thus a clear picture of some peaceful and sunny Russian landscape or village scene—remains fixed in the hearer's mind. The second movement is a picturesque and quaintly-coloured little march, which once more gives that impression of unity and logical evolution that is characteristic of Tchaikovsky at his best. The *Scherzo* is altogether charming in its vivacity, and typically Russian by reason of the irregularity of its rhythmic periods. The contrasting *Trio* is rather puerile, though not without a certain piquancy, especially when in the *coda* its 2-4 rhythm is combined with the 3-4 measure of the *Scherzo*. The *Finale*, ushered in by an introduction of which Cui said, not inaptly, that it was "as pompously trivial as the introduction to a *pas de deux*," leads to a racy Russian dance based on a folk-song known as "The Crane." It is treated quite in the modern Russian manner, with suggestions even of the whole-tone scale, and thus frequently presages such things as the dances in Rimsky-Korsakov's "Snegourotchka." The second subject is weak, but never gains the upper hand for long, the exuberant main theme being almost continually in evidence in a variety of charming versions. But, as usual, Tchaikovsky cannot leave off when he has nothing more to say; the theme is worked into a final *presto* that is, in Cui's words, "beneath all criticism."

The third Symphony (Op. 29, in D major) was composed in 1875 and first performed in Moscow during the same year. On November 12th, Tchaikovsky wrote to Rimsky-Korsakov: "It seems to me the work does not contain any very happy ideas; but, as regards form, it is a step in advance." After a hearing in St. Petersburg, Cui expressed himself more leniently than he had done on the subject of the second Symphony; and it is true that in many respects the later work is more interesting, but it comes so much nearer the feeling of the last three Symphonies that it is impossible to avoid a comparison which must inevitably lead to an unfavourable verdict. The music is no longer national—it is pure Tchaikovsky ; and there is already a strong tendency towards that subjectiveness which comes increasingly into evidence in the three later works, where the composer no longer seeks to stir our emotions but bids us give ear to his own.

The work opens with a gloomy, funereal introduction which gradually grows brighter and more animated : a fine broad sunrise effect. The principal subject then bursts forth and a concise, swift exposition of the incisive thematic material follows ; but the impressive initial effect is spoilt by over-development, and the *Coda* once again is very empty. So is the opening section of the second movement, labelled *alla tedesca*, a piece in the best manner of a German band.* Tchaikovsky, somewhere in his correspondence, points out that this Symphony has two *Scherzi*, of which this is the first. The *Trio*, with its animated chatter of the wood-wind, is very attractive, though of the slenderest musical value, and the point at which the *Scherzo* is resumed before the *Trio* is ended is dexterously

* The directors of the Vienna Philharmonic Concerts refused to allow Richter to perform the work on the ground that it was "too Russian."

brought home. The *andante elegiaco* is by no means unpleasant or unmusical, though its tragic note nowhere reaches a deep or noble degree of grief, and is soon forgotten in the vivacity of the second *Scherzo*—a mildly charming movement. The *Finale*, a bombastic *polonaise*, is the weakest portion of the work. The principal subject is commonplace and elaborated with merciless persistence. Its rhythm, constantly repeated, save for the brief and hardly edifying respite granted by the second subject and some auxiliary passages, assumes the obsessing evil fascination of the pattern of a bedroom wall-paper, which our waking fancy makes us weave into many futile combinations. As in the two preceding Symphonies the final climax is completely devoid of any meaning.

On the whole, except as curiosities, these three early Symphonies had better continue to enjoy their well-deserved rest ; but the second would be worth an occasional revival, not so much for its intrinsic musical value as for the reason that it reveals a side of Tchaikovsky entirely different from that to which we are but too much accustomed.

XV. CESAR FRANCK'S WEAKNESS

M

XV. CESAR FRANCK'S WEAKNESS

THE examination of a branch of a great composer's work that glaringly reveals the weakest aspect of his genius, does not always do him the amount of harm which such an apparently ungracious practice would seem to involve. Those who love the Symphony, the Violin Sonata, the "Variations Symphoniques" and other works that make César Franck illustrious for all time, need not be afraid to know him at his worst, for his very deficiencies are not without a certain lovable attractiveness, which enhances the greatness of the best of his work.

Franck's most serious defect is not a musical defect at all: it is his almost total lack of any sort of literary culture. Perhaps, from the musician's point of view, this may be interpreted as an advantage, since it made him pour the best in him into a form of art that was most absolutely and exclusively musical—a form so spiritually exalted as he might not have been able to evolve had he ever been engrossed with worldly or literary preoccupations. If we select a dozen or so of Franck's best works, separating the purely musical ones from those based on a literary subject, we shall find that of any two that can be opposed to each other as being in a sense parallel, the one belonging to the former class is invariably the greater. Thus, of his two finest religious works, the three Chorales for organ are more consistently good than the " Beatitudes " ; in the domain of the orchestra, the Symphony is greatly superior to " Le Chasseur maudit " ; and the " Variations Symphoniques " for piano and orchestra have every advantage over " Les Djinns " for the same combination.

Whenever Franck was confronted with the choice of a libretto or a poem, he floundered indiscriminately into whatever happened to be at hand. With religious subjects, indeed, he was less unfortunate, for his childlike, implicit faith usually guided him to some Scriptural theme that was at least congenial to his nature, if not always judiciously selected. But even here he occasionally went astray, as we may judge from those portions in the " Beatitudes " which deal with evil. Innocent and unsuspecting, aloof from the world on his organ-bench, busy among his pupils, or working at home in his spare hours, the kindly, gentle master did not succeed in depicting iniquity as anything to be taken more seriously than the devil in a pantomime. He was, perhaps, too good a man to be an artist of the first magnitude in all he attempted. In his saintly, sheltered existence, he was rather apt to miss acquiring that universal understanding and enlightenment which alone can give humanity and tenderness to art. The worldly, even the wicked, is often capable of greater sympathy than the saint. Did not Marcus Aurelius, one of the best of men, persecute the Christians, while his worthless son, Commodus, left them in peace ?

For the most convincing proof of Franck's lack of literary taste we must turn to his songs. Although once or twice he chanced by accident to light upon a good poem, the collection as a whole presents a miscellany of such appalling mediocrity that one can but sit and wonder how so fastidious a musician could have been so utterly devoid of any sort of feeling for literature. But let us be just : as a musician he was so sensitive that he could not rise to greatness where the poem he had chosen to set was inferior in quality, even though he may have sincerely believed that he liked it. We shall detect in him a remarkable felicity in descending to the level of the words selected. It was probably a matter of instinct rather than of conscious delicacy. Franck's literary taste was neither good nor bad : he simply had no taste of any kind ; but he was, after all, an artist, and his musical inspiration must have adjusted itself, unknown to him, to the value or lack of value, of his words. Goldsmith once said that, if an author chose to write a fable about little fishes, he must make them talk like little fishes ; Franck at any rate did not, as Goldsmith accused Johnson of being likely to do, make them talk like whales.

Only three great poets were drawn upon by Franck : Chateaubriand, Hugo and Musset, and they are by no means generously treated, although the setting of " Souvenance " by the first-named, a lovely nostalgic poem by one who knew the hopeless longings of an exile, belongs to his finest songs. Even so, a less easily contented composer would probably not have found it difficult to choose a poem of Chateaubriand's without such a deplorable line as this : " Who will give me back my Helen."* Next comes a literary man, whose name probably impressed Franck, but who has done nothing worth remembering—in poetry, let us add with some reluctance—Dumas.† The serenely melancholy Sully-Prudhomme happens to be represented by one of his finest poems, " Le Vase brisé." The rest is taken from various minor and obscure poets, including the amorous and quarrelsome adventurer, Joseph Méry, the one-time fashionable but now obsolete Jean-Pierre de Florian, and the baker's apprentice and solicitor's clerk, Jean Reboul, who was patronized by Lamartine and to whose " L'Ange et l'Enfant," modelled on Grillparzer, Franck wrote a pure but rather insipid melody, accompanied by a placidly trickling semiquaver figure that becomes very tiresome long before the end. M. Vincent d'Indy is quite right when he says, in connection

* " Qui me rendra mon Hélène."

† From the date (1843), obviously the elder.

with this song, that " it would be difficult to find a more intimate communion of thought between poet and musician " ; the thought, in fact, is indifferent on both sides. Yet, in comparison with some others, this song is good ; its declamation is perfect, which is not always the case elsewhere. In Alfred de Musset's " Ninon," for instance, there are some lamentable accentuations on mute syllables, the composer ruining the rhythm of the poem for the sake of a rhythm of his own, which is very charming in itself, but entirely at cross-purposes with the words, because it is thought instrumentally, not vocally. Again, in Victor Hugo's " Passez, passez toujours " there are some hideous distortions of the metre of the three verses, which, moreover, are all treated alike, with the result that the refrain becomes attenuated at each repetition instead of moving on to a climax. But the worst of the songs is the setting of Méry's " Aimer," a poem which in its fatuous ineptitude (" Aimons pour vivre et vivons pour aimer ") reminds one of the duet between Pamina and Papageno. It is run close by Florian's sentimental mock-Scotch ballad, " Robin Gray," although this is saved by some charming pastoral music, just as Méry's " L'Emir de Bengador " is saved by its pretty serenading mood. But how completely Franck gives the poet away by unconsciously writing down to his level! Méry's affectation of oriental passion is mercilessly exposed by the mediocrity of the music as the feeble, insincere trifling it is.

Three other songs of no more than tolerable value are " Le Mariage des Roses " (Eugène David), " Lied " (Lucien Paté), and " Le Sylphe " (Dumas), the latter with 'cello obbligato. They might have been written by any of the numerous third-rate French composers of the period who exploited the half-baked culture of a sentimental public. But Franck, not knowing himself what was good and what was not, cannot be accused of any such practice. Yet when for once he chanced upon a poem that was worthy of him, he instinctively invested it with music that is good to listen to. The Sully-Prudhomme example, with its finely restrained dramatic intensity, has already been mentioned, and the setting of Victor Hugo's " Roses et Papillons " has a subtle charm that might be attributed to a French master who has given his best in the domain in which Franck was weakest—Gabriel Fauré.

The words of the three songs which have had the greatest success are, at any rate, passable. " La Procession " (Ch. Brizeux), though rather superficially pictorial, certainly has much of Franck's individual flavour ; " Les Cloches du Soir " (Mme. Desbordes-Valmore) is no less typically Franckish and has some exquisite passages ; but the best song of all, and the one which discriminating singers will always select if they wish to include a really representative example of the composer in their programmes, is the " Nocturne " (L. de Fourcaud). It has a lovely vocal line, which three times takes the same turn to a cunningly varied accompaniment, and then suddenly transforms itself into a new shape. Its distinctive harmonic texture, too, is of the purest Franck, and as fine in its way as the String Quartet or the " Prelude, Chorale and Fugue." It is the only example in which the composer for once transcends the poet, and it shows that the musician in him could have given to the world vocal music of the same value as that of the best of his instrumental works, had he not been carried away by literary impressions that would have left a more fastidious artist unresponsive. The man who, during the siege of Paris, could be tricked by the enthusiasm of the hour into converting a fulsome patriotic newspaper article into a musical work* (mercifully forgotten until it was published during the Great War in a similar moment of injudicious fervour), could not be expected, even in a less febrile state of mind, to know what it was he really needed to inspire a vocal masterpiece in him. His songs show conclusively that he completely lacked all literary discrimination, a fact which is worth establishing, since it proves that it was sheer incompetence of judgment and

* " Paris," Patriotic Ode (November, 1870).

not deliberation that made him occasionally indulge the public with sentimental commonplaces. He was never insincere, and one might say of him—" if it was not such an awful thing to say of anybody," as Butler puts it—that he always " meant well " where his art was concerned. Unfortunately for posterity, his good intentions were not matched by insight when it was a question of finding good poetry for the making of songs.

XVI. THE TRAGEDY OF A COMIC OPERA

XVI. THE TRAGEDY OF A COMIC OPERA

ON May 18th, 1887, the Opéra Comique in Paris produced "Le Roi malgré lui," by Emmanuel Chabrier. A week later, after three performances, the theatre was burnt down, and a work which otherwise might have established itself at once in the public's favour was doomed to oblivion. When it was revived six months later at the Théatre Lyrique, where the performances of the Opéra Comique had been temporarily transferred, other attractions had in the meantime alienated a fickle public from an opera that deserved greater constancy. It is true that some defects of the work itself must, even under more favourable circumstances, have militated against its complete success. That Chabrier had been attracted by the subject of the play by Ancelot, one of the most successful French playwrights of the first half of the nineteenth century, on which the libretto is based, is hardly surprising, for it holds possibilities for a display of just the kind of irony and high spirits that astonishing and shamefully neglected composer knew so perfectly how to express in music; but it was one of the many disappointments of his life that he never succeeded in finding a librettist who could give him an adequate foil for his inspiration. All that can be said in favour of the libretto by Emile de Najac and Paul Burani is that the stage situations are dexterously handled and reveal a sense of variety and climax that is at any rate not below the average. For the rest, the lyrics are insipid and conventional, often descending to the cheapest platitudes, while the flatness and dullness of the dialogue is intensified by some pathetically futile efforts at humour.

The opera deals with an episode in the life of Henry III of France, the last of the Valois, who, through the influence of his mother, Catherine de Medici, and before his accession to the French throne, became King of Poland in 1574, the monarchy of that country having become elective after the extinction of the dynasty of the Jagellons.

Henry of Valois is "king against his will." He has no sooner arrived in his kingdom—unknown as yet to any of his subjects except his chamberlain, the Duke of Fritelli—than he begins to pine for his native country. On hearing that there is a conspiracy on foot against him among the Polish nobility, headed by the Count Palatine Laski, and that no more violent measures are to be adopted than to send him quietly out of the country in order to establish the Austrian pretender on the throne, he is delighted at the prospect of returning to France without incurring his mother's displeasure. It is a slave-girl of Laski's, Minka, who has disclosed

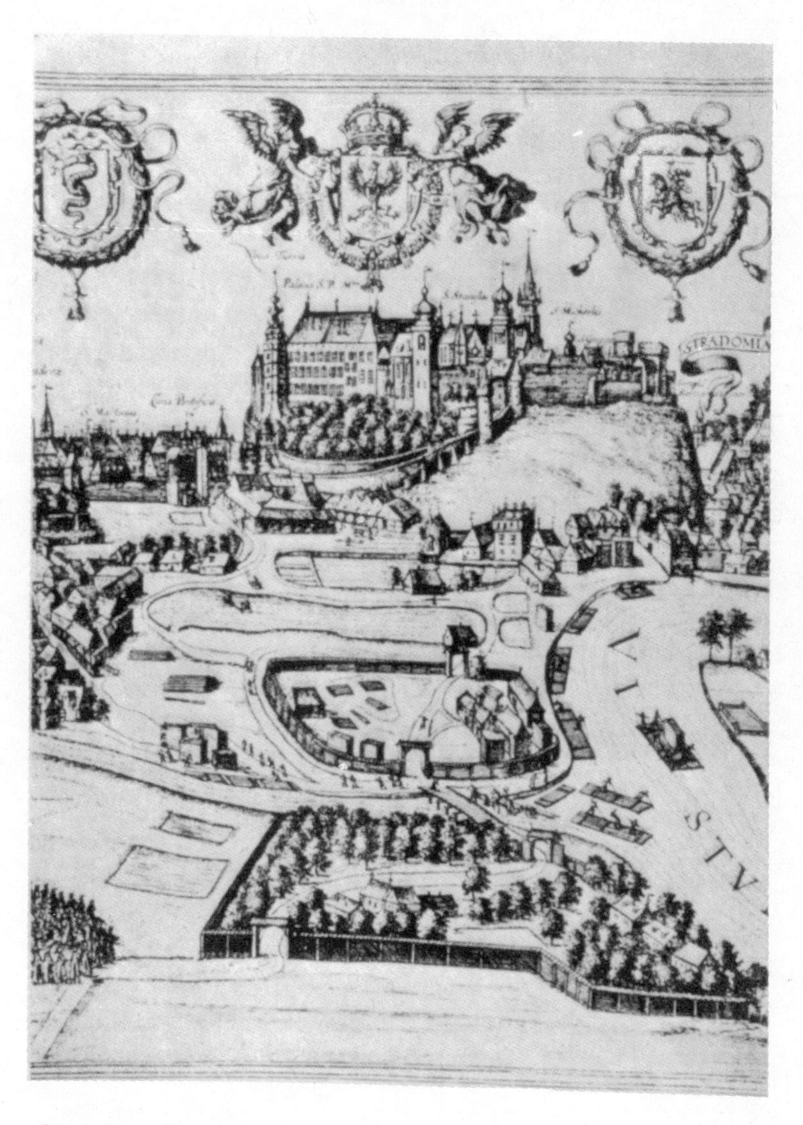

ROYAL PALACE AT CRACOW 16th CENTURY.

the plot, because she loves, and is loved by, Henry's most intimate friend, the Count de Nangis. Neither Nangis nor any of the king's retinue are aware of the fact that the unwilling monarch, far from wishing to frustrate the conspiracy, is interested in its success; and Nangis is not a little astonished when the king suddenly has him arrested without vouchsafing any explanation. Henry's plan is to give himself out as Nangis, the rumour of whose unjust treatment spreads apace, and to take part in the conspiracy under the pretext of revenging himself on the king for his imprisonment, from which he pretends to have escaped. But the situation is complicated by the fact that the Duchess of Fritelli, one of the moving spirits of the plot, recognizes in Henry an anonymous lover whom she met at Venice, and by the bursting in at the critical moment of the conjuration of the real Nangis who has escaped from captivity. In order to save his face, the king compels Nangis to pose as the new sovereign. Minka, believing that her lover is the king, is distressed at having unwittingly betrayed him by bringing him to Laski's house, where the plot is being hatched; and her agony grows on hearing that the conspirators now find no other way out of their dilemma than by slaying the king. When at this juncture the true king, to save his friend's life, declares himself, nobody believes him. The devoted Minka, however, has found means to let Nangis escape towards the frontier; and thus Henry, on whom has fallen the task of stabbing the supposed king, finds an excuse to follow him in order (as he equivocally says) to rid the Polish nobility of their unwelcome sovereign. But he has reckoned without the Polish people, who will have none of his Austrian rival, and who at last succeed (after having discovered his identity) in bringing him back to Cracow in triumph and establishing him as "king against his will."

The plot is embellished by many subsidiary episodes which by no means contribute to its lucidity; it is in fact a tangled skein which the authors themselves have some difficulty in unravelling. One may easily imagine that in performance, where the numerous, more or less clumsy explanations and asides are likely to escape the audience, the whole intrigue must remain perfectly unintelligible. But even so the opera is still worth a revival for the sake of the delicious music Chabrier has written for it.

It is not only piquancy and fancied brilliancy that make it so irresistible; its extraordinary interest, which is far greater to-day than it can have been at the time of its first production, lies mainly in the fact that we discover in it the germs of much that we have come to look upon as belonging essentially to the French music of the present century. There is one living French musician in particular who is foreshadowed very clearly in Chabrier's music: Maurice Ravel, who has himself acknowledged the immense debt he owes to Chabrier, a composer he has always adored and with whom he has an affinity that can escape only those still far too numerous music-lovers for whom the older composer has remained nothing but a name. Not only such technical matters as the very modern chord formations and progressions in the Prelude and elsewhere, but the whole spirit, the irony and elegant buoyancy of the work are predictive of Ravel.

That a composer who was so far in advance of his period should not have been understood during his lifetime is perhaps hardly surprising. His fate in this respect has many points of resemblance with that of another pioneer: his Russian contemporary, Borodin. But while the latter was condemned as an incompetent amateur who wrote hideous discords because he did not know the rules of harmony, Chabrier was looked upon rather as an extravagant buffoon who might have written quite pleasant light music if he had refrained from indulging in what must have been considered as fantastic freaks. But his most daring innovations have now revealed themselves percisely as the harbingers of the charming conceits which delight us in modern French music. In some passages of "Le Roi malgré lui," curiously enough, there is an actual resemblance to Borodin's characteristic harmony with its delicious excursions off the key, which keep us continually speculating what the next step will lead to, and leave a fascinating impression of surprise by turning into the unexpected. The Sextet of the slave-girls and the lovely Barcarolle in the second act, as well as the Nocturne in the third, are cases in point. There is, however, a great deal more vivacity in Chabrier than in his Russian contemporary. He seldom allows himself to wax lyrical, and never sentimental. His music has, on the contrary, a buoyancy that often verges dangerously on cheapness; some of his passages have a kind of brazen tonic-and-dominant vulgarity about them, but even they are never offensive. We feel inclined to smile at them as we would at some harmlessly mischievous prank played by a high-spirited schoolboy who, for all his exuberant naughtiness, has the making of a gentleman in him. Chabrier's music is so refined as a whole that we readily forgive, if not gladly enjoy, his temporary oblivion of good manners. His errors, if errors they be, are to be attributed to occasional effusions of a vivacious temperament, not to any lack of taste. Perhaps it is only because music had become, until quite recently, so distressingly decorous that we have grown accustomed to frown upon such delightful levity, of which, after all, we find examples not only in such vulgar but lovable composers as Lecocq or Offenbach, but in the works of highly respectable masters like Domenico Scarlatti, Haydn and Mozart.

Chabrier is too essentially French to be successful in his attempt at local colour. In the brilliant Waltz and the boisterous Mazurka at the opening of the second and third acts respectively, where an endeavour to convey a Polish atmosphere is distinctly discernible, there is no more feeling of Poland than there is of Venice in the Barcarolle. Historical reconstruction there is none. Chabrier, perhaps wisely, entirely ignored the sixteenth-century environment of the plot: he is simply a nineteenth-century Frenchman with a prophetic prescience of the twentieth-century music of his country.

It was the tragic fate of "Le Roi malgré lui" to be written a quarter of a century too soon. Chabrier, after a long and hopeless struggle for recognition, which led to a terrible nervous depression, died a disappointed man. It is for our generation, who have now come abreast of his work, to avenge the tragedy of this comic opera by a full appreciation of its remarkable and very individual qualities.

XVII. IMITATION HANDEL

XVII. IMITATION HANDEL

READERS of the "The Way of All Flesh" will remember that Samuel Butler makes Ernest Pontifex—or rather himself—say that he would like modern music, if he could; that he had been trying all his life to like it, but succeeded less and less the older he grew. And on being asked where he considers modern music to begin, he says "with Sebastian Bach." That Butler obstinately cut himself off from the enjoyment of pretty nearly all music except that of the one and only composer he worshipped with a fanatical monotheism appears plainly enough from his biography, his note-books and his musical criticisms. Bach he despised for what he regarded as his "niggling" methods, to Mozart's Requiem he "did not rise warmly," "Don Giovanni" bored him, and of the G minor Symphony he spoke with indulgent benevolence, as if ready to grant its misguided admirers that it was an agreeable trifle. On one occasion he said that he did not like Beethoven's Violin Concerto at all, a view of one separate work that might pass as a peculiarity of taste of little significance, but for the fact that he compared it unfavourably with a Suite by Moszkowski. For Mendelssohn he had no use whatever, which at any rate shows that he was an original in his time, and for Wagner he nursed a bitter dislike.

Nobody who knows anything about Butler

can fail to be only too well aware that for him the be-all and end-all of music was Handel, on whom he could not forbear lavishing the most extravagant panegyrics in and out of season. Handel was for him not only "the greatest musician whom the world has ever seen," and a "greater man than Homer,"* but there was nobody within any measurable distance of him. In a letter to Miss Savage,† Butler, who about 1871 was engaged as musical critic by *The Drawing Room Gazette*, says: "I only want Handel's Oratorios. I would have said, and things of that sort, but there are no 'things of that sort' except Handel's."

Can it be wondered at that a man in this frame of mind, when he took to dabbling in composition, should have been more than content with a mere imitation of the only musical style for which he had any regard? A great writer and philosopher, and a respectable painter, Butler had no creative force to spare for the exercise of an art he only liked in a rigidly circumscribed sort of way. So far went his obsession that he was quite happy to be a small satellite in the wake of the planet which so dazzled him that he was blinded to the brightest rays from any other star. His ideal was to imitate his model as

* It will be remembered that Butler held the Odyssey to have been written by a woman.

† "Samuel Butler: a Memoir." By H. Festing-Jones. Vol. I, p. 143.

MR. HEATHERLEY'S HOLIDAY BY SAMUEL BUTLER.

closely as possible, and it does not seem to have occurred to him that it is far better to create something new and original, on however small a scale, than to adopt the manner of a great master who has long used it far more effectively and completely than an amateurish imitator can ever hope to do. Butler, however, when he wrote music, did so frankly *en dilettante:* when his bright literary genius found recreation in an exercise that meant for him no more than an intellectual dalliance, he would rather take a sort of "Mr. Heatherley's Holiday" indulging his inclination, than seek new outlooks in the open air.

The chief compositions by Samuel Butler, the words and music of which were written in collaboration with his friend, and later biographer, Mr. Henry Festing-Jones, are two works for solo voices, chorus and orchestra, "Narcissus" and "Ulysses." The present study is confined mainly to the former as being the more curious of the two, and Mr. Jones's share in the work, which is in all essentials similar to Butler's, need only be referred to in passing. "Narcissus" was published in 1888, but references to it occur in Butler's letters and note-books some years before. A private rehearsal is mentioned as early as 1886, and a year later a performance was given at his old school at Shrewsbury. "Ulysses" must have been begun during the last years of the nineteenth century, for it was this work that led Butler to the re-reading, and thus to the translation, of the Odyssey, a literary task which interrupted the composition of the oratorio for a time.

"Narcissus" is described as a dramatic cantata, though the authors were well aware that it was in reality an *oratorio buffo*. The words, in which Mr. Jones says Butler took the largest share, are written in deliberate imitation of the pompous style affected by Handel's librettist, the Rev. Thomas Morell. The subject is facetious, as the following argument, prefixed to the score, will show :

> "Narcissus, a simple shepherd, and Amaryllis, a prudent shepherdess, with companions who form the chorus, have abandoned pastoral pursuits and embarked on a course of speculation upon the Stock Exchange. This results in the loss of the hundred pounds upon which Narcissus and Amaryllis had intended to marry. Their engagement is broken off, and the condolences of the chorus end Part I. In the interval between the parts, the aunt and godmother of Narcissus has died at an advanced age, and is discovered to have been worth one hundred thousand pounds, all of which she has bequeathed to her nephew and godson. This removes the obstacle to the union with Amaryllis; but the question arises

in what securities the money is to be invested. At first he is inclined to resume his speculations and to buy Egyptian Bonds, American railways, mines, etc.; but, yielding to the advice of Amaryllis, he resolves to place the whole of it in the Three per cent. Consolidated Bank Annuities, to marry at once and to live comfortably upon the income. With the congratulations and approbation of the chorus, the work is brought to a conclusion."

As a parody the words are capital, and the adoption of pastoral characters is a subtle satire on the ridiculous convention that was already in vogue in the days of Molière, who made M. Jourdain's dancing master say that "when characters have to be made to speak in music, one must needs, for the sake of probability, go to the sheepfold." There are unlimited opportunities for musical burlesque in a solemn recitative to such words as these :

Great is the joy of wealth ; but great the care
Of knowing how to turn it to account.
In what shall I invest it ?

or in fugal chorus on the following :

How blest the prudent man, the maiden pure,
Whose income is both ample and secure ;
Arising from Consolidated Three
Per cent. Annuities paid quarterly.

The trouble is that the music to " Narcissus " is not in the least comic, at any rate not intentionally so. There are only two ways of imitating an old composer with a certain measure of success: the authors of " Narcissus " should have been as solemn and serious as Handel himself—both verbally and musically—or else they should have treated the music with the same levity as they did the words. To do the former, they lacked specific genius of a purely musical order as well as supreme technical equipment; but they might have achieved a very passably amusing parody had they whole-heartedly adopted the latter alternative. They were just a little afraid of treating their model irreverently, as the substitution of the serious title of Dramatic Cantata for that of Oratorio Buffo seems to indicate. Besides, Butler says distinctly that both he and his collaborator would have regarded poking fun at Handel as a *mauvaise plaisanterie*. Elsewhere, it is true, he defends the imputation of having laughed at his idol by retorting: " Perhaps, but surely one can laugh at a person and adore him at the same time." Here is a half-hearted confession that he really meant the work to be something of a jest, but one suspects that his defence was an afterthought suggested by the accusation. At any rate, Butler once wrote in all seriousness: " In ' Narcissus ' and ' Ulysses ' I made an attempt, the failure of which has yet to be shown, to return to the principles of Handel and take them up where he left off." Unfortunately, it is very doubtful whether Handel ever had any principles: it seems much more likely that he simply had an unfailing instinct that guided him towards the methods which suited the particular bent of his genius best. He was a man easily—though never very profoundly—influenced. His first style he borrowed from Mattheson and Keiser at Hamburg; next, in Italy, he came under the sway of Alessandro Scarlatti; and at last Purcell cast his spell upon him in England. Nevertheless, he was a proud and inflexible defender of independence, and would surely have been the first to scorn any attempt at a wholesale imitation of any man's individual manner by another.

If only Butler had not taken himself so seriously, one feels that it would have needed very little more to make a delightful small work of "Narcissus." Caricature, it is true, is an art that is seldom capable of surviving its victim, but it holds opportunities for self-expression which mere mechanical, photographic reproduction lacks. There is something mildly diverting in the association of such solemn music with the flippant libretto, but the pleasantry does not by a long way outlast the considerable length of the work.

It is difficult to determine why, in spite of the

continual opportunities for humour offered by the words, the music is so conspicuously devoid of that quality. This is perhaps mainly attributable to the fact that the broad strokes of Handel's brush, imitated in a manner that, if possible, accentuates their fresco bareness, lend themselves admirably to the expression of lofty or tragic subjects, but are ill-suited to comedy. Detail is essential to humour in all the arts, as men like Hogarth, Mozart and Dickens have shown. It is not even that the music is uniformly dull, for there are many quite pleasantly Handelian numbers in the work. Nor are Butler's technical shortcomings by any means intolerably obtrusive; for an untaught amateur—he did not begin his studies of counterpoint with Rockstro until two years after the publication of " Narcissus "—he had indeed an astonishing workmanship.*

It simply comes to this in the end: serious imitation in art is a profitless pursuit, whether it be well or ill done. Bizet was right when he wrote thus:† " It is quite understood that, if I thought I imitated Wagner, I should not write another note in my life, in spite of my admiration

* I have not ascertained how far Mr. Festing-Jones was instructed in the art of composition, the matter being scarcely relevant to this chapter which deals only indirectly with Butler's collaborator.

† Letter to his mother-in-law, Madame Halévy, May 29th, 1871.

for him. . . . It is better to work badly in one's own style than in that of others. And besides, the more beautiful the model is, the more ridiculous the imitation becomes." How one wishes that Samuel Butler had been of the same mind! He would either have left Handel alone, precisely because he idolized him, or he might, knowing that he could do him no homage by being serious about him, and no hurt by being otherwise, have copied his style, lovingly, but with that wholesome disrespect for accepted institutions which has made the greatness of his "Erewhon" and "The Way of All Flesh."

XVIII. THE FATHER OF SPANISH MUSIC-DRAMA

XVIII. THE FATHER OF SPANISH MUSIC-DRAMA

TO be the originator of a movement has its tragedy as well as its glory. It takes a serious, unegotistic, ideal-minded scholar such as Felipe Pedrell, the father of the modern Spanish school, to endure calmly the mortification of the comparative obscurity, illumined by faint rays of a glory that is mainly the reflex of other people's successes, which has ever been the leader's lot in music. Pedrell, who was born in 1841 at Tortosa in Catalonia, came a generation ahead of those destined to profit, not only by the adoption of his sound principles, but also by the avoidance of his failings. And when he retired, in proud disillusionment, to his native province, he already found himself fallen a generation behind his time, his teaching usurped and improved upon by others, foremost among them Albeniz, Granados and Manuel de Falla. He had, with too self-sacrificing a generosity, bestowed his inheritance long before his decease.

It was Pedrell's patient scholarship that enabled him to lay the foundation-stone of a truly national Spanish music on the basis of its rich treasury of folk-music; it was he who bequeathed his knowledge to his juniors by means of direct teaching and valuable literary work, a bequest that was to accumulate a vast interest in their hands. But his own achievements, never known but to a few curious specialists outside the confines of his country, are already being forgotten even there in the flush of the growing glory of the new school he created.

Pedrell's operatic output is not inconsiderable, but it would serve no useful purpose to deal here with more than his most important, and at the same time most accessible, works for the stage. The earlier Operas, "El Ultimo Abencerrajo," "Quasimodo," "El Tasso a Ferrara," "Cleopatra" and "Mazeppa," produced at Barcelona and Madrid in the seventies and eighties of the last century, when they were hailed with an evanescent patriotic enthusiasm, only to be swiftly thrust off the boards by the conventional Italian repertory, embody the composer's principles in but a tentative way. The present study is therefore limited to three of Pedrell's dramatic works where both his peculiar gifts and his limitations are in full view.

There is a sentence by P. Antonio Eximeno prefixed as motto to Pedrell's pamphlet "Por nuestra Música"*: "Each country must establish its musical system on the basis of national song," which summarizes the composer's creed—a creed that incessantly occupied him, and indeed almost amounted to an obsession calculated to check the spontaneity of his invention. For it must be confessed that, although his idiom, based as it

* Published in 1891.

Felipe Pedrell

is on unfamiliar methods, seems novel enough on first acquaintance, in reality, like all preoccupations that grow into a system, it is as pedantic in its way as that which clings to the current academic rules. Pedrell was consciously, laboriously Spanish; his Hispanicisms were too much the product of erudition to be wholly convincing as a living expression: hence the fact that his glory lies so much more in what he induced in others than in what he produced himself. His was the disheartening fate of a Dargomijsky, of a Moniuszko, of every awakener of national consciousness in a musical race: the immense labour, the fierce struggle demanded by his task left him exhausted when it came to applying his discoveries to creative effort.

Pedrell's mission involved him in an enormous expenditure of time and energy, for there is not a more complex folk-music than that of Spain, which to disentangle and systematize the devoted octogenarian musician's life was hardly long enough. The country's chequered history, its mingled races, the diversity of its climes and landscapes, evolved a popular music full of varying shades of expression, and an analysis of all its tunes entails the removal of layer upon layer of characteristic features of frequently very remote and obscure origin. There are the powerful Oriental influences attendant on the Moorish invasion; the great Spanish school of church composers, who had an enormous hold on the populace; the narrative songs of the Catalan-Provençal minstrels, which are shot with Eastern elements dating from the Crusades; the ecclesiastical chant of Calvados, before the adoption of the Roman liturgy; the plain chant of the latter; Basque, Corsican, Italian, Arab, even Turkish influences; and much else beside. All these elements, almost inextricably blended in the course of time, Pedrell sought to dissect and use as separate entities on which to base his personal inspiration.* How far he succeeded in realizing his theories, a study of the scores of " Los Pirineos," " La Celestina " and " El Comte Arnau " will do enough to reveal.

" Los Pirineos " is the first drama of a great national trilogy which also includes " La Celestina " and " Raimondo Lulio,"† the three works being based respectively on the conceptions of patriotism, love and faith. There is no other connecting link between them, however, and they are in reality entirely separate works, vastly differing, not only in subject, but in style. " Los Pirineos " is based on a drama written by the Catalan poet, Victor Balaguer, in his native dialect, a language derived from the *langue d'oc*

* Direct evidence of Pedrell's learned research is to be found in his invaluable collections of folk-songs and in his splendid editions of the church music of Victoria, Morales, Cabezon and others.

† The last has remained unpublished.

which Pedrell considered as the most musical in the world. The opera is on a very ambitious scale, with a scenic setting almost as grandly impossible as that of Thomas Hardy's "Dynasts." The action takes place in the Pyrenees between the years 1218 and 1285, and is concerned with the freedom of Provence, menaced by France and Rome, and finally ensured by the heroism of the people and their devotion to the memory of the Counts of Foix.

It is no doubt this imposing setting, combined with the use of the *Leitmotiv*, that is responsible for the accusation, often levelled at Pedrell, of being too strongly tainted with Wagnerian influence, an assertion that is based on the most superficial observation. It is true that the Spanish master's themes have a certain magniloquence that reminds one of Wagner's parade heroics, but there the resemblance ends. The actual invention of the material is more like Liszt's, the method of presenting it more like Rimsky-Korsakov's, the declamation more like Moussorgsky's, if comparisons must needs be drawn. Even the *Leitmotiv* is used by Pedrell in a way that is not Wagner's: less strictly logical in theory, it is at times more to the purpose in practice. Instead of actually accompanying a character or the reference to a character, it sometimes occurs when the personage it is attached to is neither present nor even mentioned, as in the case, to point to a single example, of the legate from Rome, who only appears at the end of the first act, but whose sinister theme is heard before the libretto hints at the part he is about to play. Again, Pedrell does not handle the dialogue in the manner of a spoken drama, but frequently allows it to overlap, using vocal combinations to a considerable extent, thus marking the essential difference between opera and drama and adhering to a style of real "music-drama" instead of merely retarding the action of a fully developed spoken drama by music that is not strictly necessary to its completeness. At the same time, although the dialogue is sufficiently compressed, the whole plan of the work is too spacious, inordinate lengths being produced by a wealth of matter that is scarcely relevant, and certainly not essential, to the unfolding of the drama. The whole long prologue, strictly speaking, is superfluous, although as a kind of *symphonic* summary of the whole play in a mystic-archaic atmosphere gained by copious use of old Spanish church music it has its interest. As regards form, "Los Pirineos" presents no new features: there are the conventional separate operatic "numbers," connected by recitative and slightly disintegrated by the *Leitmotiv* system. Nor has the composer a very strong power of spinning out his musical material. He too often stretches it beyond endurance by sheer repetition, and frequently creates a sense of development by false pretences, much as Rimsky-Korsakov does, by merely restating a passage in a new key and with altered scoring. His climaxes are generally built up by the conventional use of long *crescendi*, pedal-points and the like, while for dramatic effects he relies on the usual frenzied tremolos and over-emphatic restatements of some theme or another.

All these weaknesses may well induce one to ask whether Pedrell was a sufficiently powerful composer to realize his ideals, and not merely a reformer unable to practise what he preached—whether he was not another Cesar Cui. The truth is that his suggestions of reform did not embrace the whole problem of the music-drama; that beyond the adoption of a national Spanish musical idiom he brought no new element into dramatic music. But as far as he set out to go, he undoubtedly went. Pedrell spoke the language of his country in every note he wrote. He did it too consciously, too scholastically, but he did it completely. It is true that to the ordinary cultured European his music does not sound particularly Spanish, but then we have not yet come to recognize as typically Iberian any other of the numerous elements that went to the making of Spanish music beyond those which are based on Oriental influences, too often watered down for us by superficially cultured cosmopolitan musicians, and presented by them as genuine. What would strike the average hearer as the most *Spanish* piece in "Los Pirinoes" is the *Moorish* song in the first act, yet any passage in the opera, picked out indiscriminately, is equally representative of some aspect or another of the country's folk-music.

"La Celestina," although written in the same vein, is distinctly inferior to "Los Pirineos" in subject-matter and construction. To begin with, the libretto, adapted by the composer from a tragic love-story by Fernando de Rojas, is very feeble dramatically, though full of picturesque incidents, many of which—long-winded and irrelevant as they are—at any rate provide an excellent excuse for some splendid music in Pedrell's native idiom. The chief fault of the plot lies in the fact that nearly every catastrophe is brought about by causes that do not of necessity arise out of the action. Again, the characters continually explain themselves to the audience and to each other, and we are too often told over again what we have just witnessed on the stage—a truly Wagnerian touch at last! The *Leitmotiv* is much more assiduously used in this work than in "Los Pirineos," and the hearer's patience is apt to be severely tried towards the end by the merciless restatement of the same themes with far too little variation. The whole work is a counterpane made up of various bright patches, stitched together with a maddening regularity of repetition, and too thinly padded with real substance to yield enough warmth.

A very different work again is "El Comte Arnau," hardly an opera at all, but rather a dramatic cantata with two choruses, one active, the other narrative. The libretto, a fine dramatic poem, based on the popular Catalan ballad of Count Arnau, a figure that blends the character of Don Juan with the fate of the Flying Dutchman, is by Juan Maragall. This is the most distinctive dramatic work of Pedrell's as regards form,* the most concise, swift and direct, and the one which most completely expresses his personality. Nothing but a loosely-strung sequence of detached scenes, almost cinematographic in appearance, it nevertheless hastens on rapidly to a tragic climax and to a kind of final apotheosis which forms a culmination that is deeply musical by nature. The work suffers from the same scrappy method of construction as "La Celestina," but in a lesser degree, the patches being cut to a larger scale and the thematic invention more individually coloured and forcible. In any case, its good qualities more than overbalance its minor defects.

There may scarcely be any interest in producing one of Pedrell's other music-dramas, although they will long remain worth studying at home,

* "El Comte Arnau" can be performed equally well in the concert room, on the stage, or in the open air.

but a performance of "El Comte Arnau," especially in concert form, is perfectly practicable and would be an undertaking of real interest, not a mere pious tribute to a composer who laboured hard and with touching devotion at the renascence of his country's national music.

XIX. MAX REGER AT THE ORGAN

XIX. MAX REGER AT THE ORGAN

THE exclusive study of one particular branch of a composer's output seldom makes for a satisfactory estimate of his personality. It would be grossly unfair to Beethoven to judge him by his songs alone, and Wagner would not have a leg to stand on if his non-dramatic works alone were considered. But it is sometimes profitable to look at the aspect of a man's work that shows him at his weakest; it is a salutary counteraction to a sentimental hero-worship often based on blind infatuation for one or two isolated works or on national prejudice. Conversely, when a composer is by common consent relegated to disregard, more likely than not because he may have been injudiciously introduced by a few works that do not represent the best side of him, it is only equitable, before condemning him finally, to establish a case for his defence by examining once more the facts that place him in the most favourable light.

Max Reger has, outside Germany, where the public still desperately clings to him as a possible perpetuator of the classicism that has slipped from that country's grasp, never taken a foothold, precisely because of his adherence to these ideals. The world at large has never taken him for a composer with anything more vital to do than the filling of old moulds with new matter, and it seems strange how anybody but those who deliberately close their eyes to an uncomfortable truth could have been deceived by his crabbed chromaticism and his jerky modulations into the illusion that even this matter presented anything really novel. There was, therefore, good reason for Reger's failing to impose himself on any country but his own, for no musician has ever been known to achieve a world-wide reputation by a mere attachment to tradition, unless he had, like Brahms, a distinctly personal language in which to express established formulas. At the same time, Reger has frequently been condemned on circumstantial evidence—criticism in his case has been largely based, by deduction, on the hearing of one or two isolated works. In order to make sure that he has not been unjustly convicted, it may be thought worth while to examine once more an aspect of his art that undoubtedly presents him at his best. It is his organ music that we shall have to turn to if we wish to study that portion of his work which is likely to prove the most enduring.

Max Reger learned to play the organ in his boyhood, and he always had a great predilection for an instrument which has been exceedingly shabbily treated throughout musical history. Of the great composers only two or three made a systematic study of it, the others leaving it

DRAWING BY HOENISCH, 1910.

Max Reger

to the mercy of the specialists, many of whom, although they knew its capabilities and how to turn them to account effectively, unfortunately did not happen to be composers of the first rank. It must be admitted that Reger's organ works, which take up a considerable portion of his production, profit to some extent by the fact that this instrument has been so consistently neglected; by comparison with the trash that has been so profusely poured out by more or less able organists, it is lifted to a somewhat more exalted level than would be its due if there were as much great organ music to compare with it as there is orchestral, piano or vocal music. Yet it is not difficult to see that this department of Reger's work contains not only relatively, but positively, the best he had to give.

To begin with, Reger knew, and brilliantly exploited, all the resources of the organ so far as they were known up to his time. The enormous difficulties of the larger works show that he, at any rate, did his share to improve the instrument's technique, and that he was wise enough to place his music beyond the reach of the incompetent ; but he opened up none of the new possibilities of colour and texture which still lie stored up in this wonderfully resourceful instrument and remain as yet icebound by the contrapuntal traditions established by Bach. Reger, for all his intimacy with the organ, was too tied up in his veneration for that master to realize that his style is capable of no expansion. Bach did the greatest things that can possibly be done in his own manner; his work for the organ is a glorious fruit grown out of the seeds and blossoms of his predecessors, a fruit which, fully ripened in his charge, can only decay in the hands of those who endeavour to develop it further. The great composer is yet to come who shall at last wake up to the fact that the organ is not really an ideal polyphonic instrument at all. No man has so far appeared who has refused to let himself be blinded to this truth by the genius of Bach, who wrote organ music in a polyphonic style simply because he happened to be a great contrapuntist as well as a great organist. And this was but one of a series of historical accidents whereby the organ became the vehicle for a mode of expression for which it is by no means ideally fitted. It is true that many of the smaller organist-composers have, perhaps instinctively, come to the conclusion that their instrument is far more suitable for a homophonic style with vertical chord-sequences; but none of them have been able to convince musicians of the fact, because their works have shrunk into insignificance beside the great polyphonic writers as far as sheer musical import goes. So we are still awaiting the master who shall initiate us into the modern use of the organ.

REGER AT THE ORGAN

It was hardly to be expected of Reger, who never shone as an innovator, that he should make the discovery of such new possibilities in the organ. He was content to deal with accepted resources which, it must be allowed, are appropriate enough to the ideas they express. His astounding erudition and polyphonic facility, moreover, make of him a more interesting figure as a follower than he could ever have succeeded in being as a leader.

Everything in Reger's organ music comes from Bach, sometimes, as may be judged from a certain sleekness of the texture, by way of Mendelssohn, but more often in a direct line. The very moulds into which the younger composer pours the ready flow of his invention are those of the older master—Chorale Preludes, Fantasies on German hymn tunes, and the inevitable Fantasy and Fugue on B A C H. Nor does the treatment differ in any essential from that of Bach, while the idiom is the strangest mixture of actual imitation and a translation of accustomed terms into a new language. Innumerable are the phrases that sound like passages of familiar poetry, originally written in a virile, living tongue, but now transcribed into the colourless, invertebrate Esperanto. Never by any chance does this music strike one, in spite of all its shifting chromaticisms, as modern in the true sense of the term. There is not a single chord whose combination defies the analysis of the textbook; all the harmonies, taken separately, belong to the comparatively limited number of orthodox chords, and it is only the unexpected manner of their sequence that lends them a superficial appearance of strangeness. Where there is an apparent foreign admixture, it is in the nature of a suspension that can always be resolved into an accepted compound. There is no vestige of that sense of harmonic "colour" that is one of the greatest acquisitions of the moderns. Reger's harmony is all patchwork which never succeeds in sustaining a distinct mood for any length of time. But if he fails as a colourist, he is a designer of great forms who knows his business when it is a question of building up vast architectural structures. Here, in his old-fashioned way and from his own point of view, the advantage is his. Such things as the Sonatas, the work on the name of "Bach," and the Symphonic Fantasy and Fugue (Op. 57)—due allowance being made for their characteristic defects—are fine examples of their kind; they may be accepted as splendidly monumental and impressive utilizations of conventional patterns. It is only when we remember how they and their like have succeeded in deceiving musicians by their sham modernity into representing their composer as a daring iconoclast that they irritate us to such a degree that we are apt to forget their great qualities.

REGER AT THE ORGAN

The same love of established usage, under a still thinner veneer of novelty, is to be found in the Chorale Preludes and the Fantasies on hymn tunes, where long patches of open and unabashed imitation of Bach are on the whole far better and more convincing than those passages where one is conscious of an insincere attempt on the composer's part to express ideas by means of a personal language. Whenever Reger waxes chromatic after his own way he at once loses all spontaneity and becomes a scientist holding forth in the driest possible manner on the carcase he dissects. The exposition of the chorales that are full of magnificent force and the fugues that open in a vein of splendid vitality always have a more or less unadulterated Bach flavour; as soon as they go off into sheer Reger there is an uncomfortable feeling that a conscious attempt at originality and an effort to keep up the continuity is being strained to a breaking point.

The greatest virtue of Reger's organ music, as compared with the rest of his work, is the total absence of that sickly, beery sentimentality that makes many of his songs and piano pieces so insufferable. This emotional restraint lifts him to a higher plane as a composer for the organ, for all his dryness and lack of personality. But he is at his best only interesting as an antiquarian. It is a particularly cynical jest on the part of musical history to have turned Max Reger, who not many years ago shocked Germany by his mock audacities, into a composer who to-day and outside his own country is only tolerable where he is most conservative.

XX. THE CHAMBER MUSIC OF ALBERT ROUSSEL

XX. THE CHAMBER MUSIC OF ALBERT ROUSSEL

IF the modern French school has not contributed an overwhelming number of immortal works to the literature of chamber music, it must at any rate be credited with having done a thing that was sorely needed: it has opened the windows of the chamber to let in fresh air and sunlight, and it has swept away the cobwebs and stuffy atmosphere of academicism, which had by no means disturbed the assembly of German professors and their disciples who occupied the place and jealously guarded the redolence of staleness that hung about it. Nobody attached sufficient importance to the small group of enterprising young people from Paris, who had burst in among the frock-coats of formality clad in the loose and cosy velvet jacket of the unfettered artist, to oppose them seriously or even to notice them, until it was found that they had turned the house out of doors and that it was too late to remonstrate. One of these disrespectful intruders—and by no means the least adventurous—was Albert Roussel, who in 1894 decided (at the age of twenty-five) to abandon a naval career in order to devote himself entirely to music.

The first work contributed to chamber music by Roussel is the Trio (Op. 2) for piano, violin and 'cello, a work in which we can trace at once a spirit of freedom and the healthy, breezy feeling of the sea, combined necessarily with an immaturity of style and a certain lack of polish which is, however, anything but unpleasant to those who prefer the plain speech of a child of the open air to the carefully weighed rhetoric of the scholar. This Trio wavers curiously between an anxious clinging to and an utter abandonment of formality, as if the composer had not felt safe in deciding on either course. The result is a compromise between a classical sonata that shows traces of the cyclic form of the Franck school and a complete renunciation of any kind of precedent. The work makes one think of a high-spirited young person who endeavours to realize modern ideas of dress by a loose adaptation of various old-fashioned garments. Yet, though the attempt be only partly successful, it is refreshing to see a young composer striving to prove that chamber music, in spite of its name that suggests the interior, need not be pent up within four walls; and who, though he likes to listen to music indoors, sees no reason why it should not tell of the beauty of nature in all its aspects, of the changing moods of the seasons, of sunrise and sunset, of wind and rain, of mist or of storm. It is the presence of such things in the Trio that appeals to our imagination in spite of the remnants of formality still clinging to it. From the hazy atmosphere of the opening page, out of which ideas of a more definite shape gradually emerge, to the close that recedes back into the mist, there are countless passages suggestive of nature. The objection that such effects are orchestral and have no legitimate place in chamber music, is a mere platitude; for if a composer succeeds in expressing mood-pictures perfectly through the medium of three instruments, he more than fully justifies the attempt. And Roussel did succeed. If there is anything in the Trio to which exception might be taken, it is not its mode of expression but the remaining vestiges of convention, such as the *stretto* at the end of the first movement and some traces of mannerisms of modernity, which often give the impression of having been arbitrarily introduced simply because the composer was anxious to make due use of the resources that had come into vogue about the time at which the work was written. The whole-tone scale, for instance, wherever it crops up, looks like the deliberate application of an artifice required by fashion rather than an inevitable means of conveying a definite mood or feeling.

The first movement is both poetical and well shaped; in fact, form and atmosphere are inseparably welded together into one unity. The lovely *coda*, where the piano sinks back into the haze of the opening while the strings give out the second subject in augmentation, is a stroke of genius and a perfect climax as regards form and feeling alike. The slow movement is the most consistently fine portion of the work. It is a song made of broad, long-drawn melodic phrases that sometimes give way to free declamation; and, in spite of the numerous changes of time, the whole is well knit and sustained in mood.

The Finale, a gay and sprightly movement is a little too discursive and indefinite to be quite on a level with what has gone before. There are many passages where the music seems to be kept going without any impelling force behind it, like an electric train that moves on after the current has been shut off. These moments alternate with patches of great inspiration, which somehow fail to unite with the rest. Nor does the cyclic form, with its reminiscences of the two preceding movements, make for repose. The very subtly introduced *coda*, however, which once again reverts to the opening mood, does much to re-establish a balance and to impart to the work a final touch of genuine poetry.

There is occasionally a faint folk-song flavour about this Trio, attributable perhaps to the fact that Roussel studied composition with Vincent d'Indy. At any rate, the cult of the folk-song seems to be scarcely anything more than another of those artificially applied resources, an assumption that is supported by the more mature Violin Sonata, Op. 11 (published in 1909),

CARICATURE BY HASSELT.

where almost every trace of a national idiom has disappeared. That is not to say that the Sonata, or for that matter the whole of Roussel's work, is not intensely French, but it has its root in the culture rather than in the soil of France.

The Violin Sonata is in a sense much more loosely built, yet it gives an impression of far greater unity than the Trio. If there is greater freedom about the later work, there is also a greater sobriety in its enjoyment. Roussel has learnt how far he can strain at the leash without cutting himself entirely loose from the traditions that always remain at the base of his work. The Sonata is a plant firmly rooted in the soil of tradition, yet thriving freely in the healthy open air; it retains nothing more than the broad outlines of usage and is no longer subject to its petty and tyrannical mannerisms. Roussel's range of emotion has considerably widened by this time, and each feeling has become deeper and more intense. The Sonata is less poetical perhaps than the Trio, but then it has not the limitations of poetry; it is a tale that tells realistically of darkling passion and vigorous joy and bitter anguish—a thing of measured, balanced prose, full of the essence of poetry but free from its metrical restrictions. The first movement is passionate, almost violent at times, and has moments of a noble eloquence which scarcely ever falls into verbosity; while the second is a light-hearted piece full of piquant, caressing humour, relieved by a slow section that introduces a note of gravity. The Finale opens vigorously in a vacillating rhythm of 5-4 alternating with common time, and the movement pursues its course with a brilliant, bustling energy that is infinitely refreshing in its unflagging vitality.

The " Divertissement " (Op. 6), for piano and wind instruments (flute, oboe, clarinet, bassoon and horn), is an earlier (1906) and comparatively unimportant work, which does not reveal the composer's personality to the same extent as the two already referred to. While both of these are representative of a very distinct individuality, this little work might have been composed by almost any French musician who has a happy knack of writing for and blending wind instruments. But the " Divertissement " makes up by charm what it lacks in personality. There is a clean pastoral feeling about it that is wholly delightful, and the absence of any weighty ideas is compensated for by delicate colour and a fine feeling for dynamic light and shade.

Since Roussel has, even in the purest forms of chamber music, successfully introduced picturesque and descriptive elements that place these works somewhere near the realm of programme music, another work must be included here in spite of its connection with the stage. This is the incidental music to G. Jean-Aubry's verse playlet, "Le Marchand de Sable qui passe," scored for flute, clarinet, horn, harp and strings. Jean-Aubry's poem in one act is couched in a form that is itself, so to speak, a literary equivalent of chamber music; it has the same intimacy, and the poetical drift of its ideas moves forward on the strength of the inner meaning instead of depending on incidents and stage situations, a process of thought that is very closely related to that which is productive of the most abstract form of music. These scenes between three persons—He, She and a figure akin to the Sandman of the fairy tales, the bringer of sleep and, with it, of dreams and their realization—are so elusive as to be outwardly almost eventless; it is what is hidden below the surface that constitutes the real action. The work is therefore, in spite of its dramatic form, absolute poetry, just as the music that adumbrates it and intensifies its feelings rather than its incidents, is really pure chamber music.

It can be—and frequently has been—performed in the concert room, where it makes up by its sheer musical charm for the loss of the deeper significance it borrows from the poetry that engendered it. There is a strange fascination in the numerous thematic strands that emerge here and there from an ethereally delicate tissue, and the physical pleasure afforded by the composer's deft and subtle handling of his miniature orchestra, from which he extracts an astonishing variety of entrancing, half-veiled and half-luminous sound-values, is alone sufficient to make the work acceptable away from the stage. This music has all the intangible and fleeting, but intense and alluring, charm suggested by the subject it was written to illustrate; it takes the hearer into a land of dreams and strange fancies. Regarded as concert music, it is too lacking in substance to leave a very strong impression, but this defect is its very virtue if it be considered that it is precisely something delicately vague and elusive that both poet and composer have successfully striven to convey.

XXI. ELGAR'S MOST NEGLECTED MASTERPIECE

XXI. ELGAR'S MOST NEGLECTED MASTERPIECE

ONLY a great master may venture to approach a worn-out musical form, for he alone can hope to extract from a stereotyped mould a shape containing a mixture of ingredients that is capable of reviving our taste for too familiar a dish. Elgar certainly succeeds in his "Falstaff"—one of his greatest works, though shamefully neglected—in rousing our interest in, and almost re-awakening our affection for, so stale a form as the symphonic poem applied to the Wagnerian principle of the "leading motive." It seemed already more than a decade ago that Strauss had ridden this chosen Bucephalus of his to death; but Elgar, on mounting its exhausted frame, summoned up some of its old strength once more and spurred it a little further ahead.

There is no doubt that "Falstaff" comes under the category of the symphonic poem, although Elgar calls it a "symphonic study," a subtle distinction that aptly describes the composer's penetration into the character he set out to portray. It is true that he does not limit himself to characterization alone, for he outlines concurrently with the protagonist's outstanding traits the chief incidents of his career. But the latter are always made subservient to the former, and their importance is carefully kept within the limits of their power to throw some light on the aspects that formed the composer's chief preoccupation. It is here that we find Elgar much more discerning than Strauss, who is generally considered as the most perfect exponent of the modern symphonic poem, and may certainly claim to be the most successful, precisely because he is more easily contented with surface aspects. While Strauss and his partisans are hugely and childishly amused by a clever imitation of bleating sheep or nagging women, things that are merely incidental and contribute nothing to the inner psychological development; and, while his realism too often follows the line of least resistance,* Elgar makes us feel that, for all his wealth of detail, he never loses sight for a moment of the effect of his picture as a whole, and never resorts to superficialities.

But if it be a question of popularity, the virtues of his symphonic poem are precisely its most serious defects. It is like a vast canvas, tremendously effective when seen at a distance, but at the same time so full of interesting detail that we are continually tempted to approach so closely as to be no longer able to take in the general impression. We are then torn between the choice of following the work with the aid of a score in order to savour the whole of its masterly crafts-

* There is nothing easier, for instance, than to suggest wind by means of a wind machine; any stage hand can do it.

manship, and of enjoying the greater æsthetic satisfaction of penetrating into the manner in which the character of the pot-bellied knight is visualized. "Falstaff," unfortunately, seems doomed to unpopularity simply because it cannot be absorbed by any hearer at one performance, and because only a minority of music lovers will take the trouble of studying the work at the piano or in the arm-chair, and of thus preparing themselves for a hearing by impressing the thematic material on their memory. We do this kind of thing for Wagner with the utmost readiness, but we refuse, by some strange and tragic perversity, to do it for Elgar. We are infinitely impressed by a master who takes four evenings to develop musically and dramatically what could easily have been said in one; but we have no respect for a genius who compresses into half-an-hour of splendid music every reference to a character contained in three of Shakespeare's historical plays and every literary commentary ever published on the subject. It may be too much to ask us to follow an erudite lecture condensed into thirty minutes of music, and at the same time to listen to a brilliant, witty and pathetic narrative and look upon a series of varied and highly coloured scenes following each other in rapid succession; but, unless we prepare ourselves for such a feast by several hours of study, the work cannot impress us as it should, and we are in great danger of losing ourselves in the contemplation of the scenery and missing the deeper significance of the play. If we are not on intimate terms with the work beforehand, its performance will strike us as nothing more than a series of scenes as loosely strung together as those of a cinematographic film, and moreover it will not be possible to follow it intelligently save with the aid of an elaborate programme that can only the more detract from the sheer loveliness of the music and the marvels of the thematic workmanship. "Falstaff," with its profusion of interesting features, makes an impression similar to the shows of the ill-fated Barnum and Bailey that delighted our childhood and distressed us by the impossibility to see all the multitudinous turns that were going on at one and the same time.

But this *embarras du choix* that perplexed our youth is nothing compared with "Falstaff's" manifold claims on our attention. The work contains so many factors of absorbing interest that we lose greatly even if we succeed in catching hold of one or two of them. There is, first and foremost, the characterization of the protagonist to be followed, a wonder of subtle observation entirely worthy of a Shakespearean subject. The themes devoted to Falstaff which, as becomes the central figure of the work, link up the whole musical structure, are so clearly appropriate as to make the different sides of this complex tragi-comic character perfectly lucid to us. The ponderous, portly principal theme is confined to Sir John's outward appearance, another shows him swaggering and attempting to cut an impressive figure, a third is descriptive of his waggish cajolery, a fourth of his inveterate bragging and lying. Round this central material are grouped the clear-cut themes of the minor characters, such as the elegant and courtly motive of Prince Henry, the flippant figure depicting the women at the Boar's Head, the rickety march of Falstaff's soldiery, and the stern, proud theme of the newly-crowned King. These personal motives are lavishly interspersed with a number of themes, as varied in aspect as they are uniform in beauty, which here elucidate the incidents of the story and there set the scenery for them. The teeming riot of the Eastcheap tavern, the stealthy, muffled commotion of the midnight adventure at Gadshill, the mellow loveliness of a Gloucestershire orchard, the pomp of Westminster on the day of the coronation, are all visualized with almost incredible precision.

The thematic material alone is enough to keep us in breathless delight for half-an-hour, and we might be satisfied by merely letting it caress our senses, were not our attention continually detracted by the fascinating modifications undergone by it as the vicissitudes of the principal character unfold themselves. The Falstaff motives are, of course, predominant throughout, and they leaven the whole musical substance. The different incidents through which they pass colour and transform them, until finally we reach the infinitely poignant but never sentimental passages of Falstaff's disgrace and death, one of those profoundly moving and truly Shakespearean revulsions from amused contempt to fierce indignation with life for having reduced a man to so pitiable a figure. Shakespeare had as great an affection for his fools, his villains, and his drunkards as he had for his heroes and lovers. Even where he makes us thoroughly despise a character for his imbecility, his wickedness or his profligacy, he has a way of enlisting, almost against our will, our sympathy with the tragedy that underlies these human defects and of making it outweigh our contempt. When Malvolio is "most notoriously abused," when the arbitrary judgment passed on Shylock proves more savage than his own cruelty, the wisest and most virtuous among us are moved to take their part. Elgar brought the most profound understanding to bear on psychological changes such as these, and his dexterity in introducing, half-way through the work, a premonitory touch of pathos in the shape of an interlude where Sir John dreams of his boyhood and of what might have been, is a master-stroke quite in the spirit

Mr. Quin in the Character of Sr. John Falstaff.

of Shakespeare, though not directly borrowed from him. Again, the distortion of the women's theme into drowsy and incoherent remembrance as Falstaff falls asleep, although more superficial, is a no less finely conceived effect; and, even when Falstaff snores, we are not moved to laughter alone, as we are by the snorts of Sancho Panza in Strauss's "Don Quixote," but also to pity for a human being, once full of bright hopes, now a fat and lewd old man, the last vestiges of whose dignity are only precariously upheld by boastful mendacity. The transformation of the shaky soldiers' march into a warm, blithe song as they approach the orchards of Gloucestershire, and the reference to the theme thus gained when the dying knight "babbles of green fields," are but other isolated examples of the many ingenious touches with which the score abounds.

But the work presents other features which peremptorily claim our attention and will not let us admire at leisure all its details. Next to the beauty of the themes, all of a typically Elgarian cut, yet so extraordinarily varied, and next to the wonderful psychological significance they assume in their development, it is the almost incredible technical skill with which they are combined that strikes us most forcibly. Apparently totally irreconcilable melodies are frequently welded together into perfect agreement, as if by some magic touch; and yet, more wonderful still, instead of covering each other up, they are distinctly and separately heard, and the desired sense of conflict is somehow preserved in spite of the perfect contrapuntal unity.

Then there is, again, the orchestration to be admired. The work is heavily scored, and the full orchestra is kept going with comparatively little respite for any of the instruments. Nethertheless, this music has nothing of the muddy thickness and of the abominable "safe" orchestration of Strauss and his school, with its everlasting doubling, trebling, and quadrupling of parts that will scarcely ever allow the unadulterated tone-quality of any instrument to be heard, and always gives the impression of several groups of instruments supporting each other lest something should go wrong in one of the parts. In Elgar's score we do hear the *timbres* of the different instruments wherever he needs them; and even when the whole orchestra is playing he can at will make any important part stand out with remarkable clarity. Nor does he resort to the Straussian paddings which artificially keep up a sort of frenzied excitement with no real passion behind it. His scoring is as full as that of any of Strauss's symphonic poems, but the fulness is of a different kind. It is a glittering, coruscating texture of short phrases, a rich carpet woven of thousands of infinitesimal strands of various colours. To work thus mosaically is, however, fraught with some dangers. It reduces the orchestral player to a figurant and makes it difficult for him to become engrossed in his work, while the demands for a close scrutiny of the workmanship and, at the same time, for a contemplation of the whole effect as it were from a distance, are too great to be complied with by the average concert-goer.

The tragedy of the lamentable non-success of " Falstaff " can only be explained by its being too great and complex a work to make at a first hearing the overwhelming impression which none who know it intimately can escape.

XXII. BELA BARTOK AS QUARTET WRITER

XXII. BELA BARTOK AS QUARTET WRITER

A GREAT deal has been written about Béla Bartók as a "national" composer. So much stress has been laid on this feature that his music, so far as it is listened to at all, is thought chiefly, if not exclusively, interesting as a modern reflection of the peculiarities of Hungarian folk-music and as a continuation of the efforts of Brahms and Liszt to catch its spirit. Bartók's claim to greatness has been too often based by his well-meaning champions on the bare fact that he succeeded better than these two masters in this particular aim ; but this is a poor compliment to pay to the younger composer if it is remembered that Liszt left Hungary at the age of ten and Brahms only knew it as a visitor. Therefore, were Bartók's reputation to rest entirely on his superiority over an unimportant side-issue of the other two composers' work, there would be small hope for his future. The mere statement that Bartók is as Hungarian as Sibelius is Finnish or Manuel de Falla Spanish cannot make a great composer of him. To do no more than to record the characteristic features of the music of one's country is not enough : a true artist has the potentiality of greatness in him long before national consciousness comes into play and colours the development of his personality.

STEPCHILDREN OF MUSIC

Béla Bartók was born a genius. It was well for the variety of the art of music that he happened to come into the world in Hungary and that he should have had access to the peasant music of his country in its original form, unspoilt by the gipsy influences that had perverted and distorted it in the versions that came into the hands of Liszt and Brahms. If Bartók had no other merit than that of having given us an insight into the true spirit of this music, it would be sufficient for us to be beholden to him, although no service of this kind alone could have long deceived us into taking him for the creator that he is. He would have been a valuable archæologist instead of an interesting composer. His later works, in fact, where national elements no longer appear practically in their original forms (as they do in such early things as the Orchestral Suite or the Rhapsody for piano and orchestra)* but are as it were filtered through his own personality, are infinitely more interesting and convincing. He has so entirely absorbed the modes of expression peculiar to his home, they are so inextricably fused with those of his individuality that it has become impossible to distinguish any dividing

* These two works, incidentally, were written before Bartók had clearly distinguished between the true Magyar peasant music and the numerous foreign elements artificially placed on Hungarian soil by political situations that did not eradicate their ethnographical peculiarities. In his later works Bartók is always careful to make it quite clear when he makes use of themes belonging to Slovak or Roumanian territories.

line : but as his extraordinarily rapid development progresses, the man's personality becomes more and more dominant. It subjects the folk-idiom to its purpose with greater ease, and the composer's thoughts, although still expressed in his native language, are lifted high enough out of all national boundaries to become universally significant.

The progress of this gradual ascendancy of individual over national expression may be most easily studied in Bartók's piano music, since this is the most accessible portion of his work. But there, even in his later pieces, he still frequently resorts to a deliberate use of actual folk-music (coloured it is true by his personal idiom), and his evolution is reflected still more clearly in his other instrumental works. From the early orchestral works just mentioned to the first String Quartet, it is but a space of three or four years ; seven or eight elapsed between this and the second Quartet (the two Images for orchestra intervening) ; and only four lie between the second Quartet and the amazing and hauntingly beautiful first violin and piano Sonata.*

The two Quartets are landmarks in this

* This has been called an ugly work, chiefly on account of the minor seconds and augmented octaves which Bartók uses as freely here as Brahms uses thirds and sixths ; but even granted that these intervals are ugly—which is after all only a question of usage—the ideas exposed by means of them are surely among the loveliest things music can be called upon to express.

development, and as such make a fascinating study in connection with Bartók's whole output ; but it is sufficient to give one's attention to them separately, as music pure and simple, to become convinced that they are the inevitable personal expression—personal confession one might almost say—of a lucid and sincere artistic mind.

Few musicians are likely to come across Bartók's String Quartets, neglected as they are, before they have become familiar with some isolated specimens at least of his piano music. They will, when they do happen to see a score or hear a performance of the Quartets, be at once struck by their difference from the composer's keyboard music. This difference is the result of his extraordinary faculty of adapting the musical texture of each work to the ways and means of its realization. There cannot be the slightest doubt that Bartók's creative impulse must produce simultaneously an intuitive knowledge of what will be the most suitable vehicle for its expression. It may be deduced therefrom that the plan of a whole work must exist in the composer's mind before he begins to write down a note of it, and this conjecture is substantiated by the irresistible impression of unity made by all his music. He does not begin with a small thematic fragment and gradually amplify it into a great structure, but on the contrary makes all the incidents subservient to the whole idea already planned out in his mind. He is never led astray by irrelevancies. Thus, although in the quartets he discards the classical sonata form,* we are nevertheless conscious of a feeling of logical evolution and continuity. Bartók achieves here the feat of arriving at the symmetry and balance needful to a great edifice, if it is not to collapse on being submitted to the test of time, by disregarding the old mathematical principles and building a masterly structure by instinct, as a bird builds its nest. Nor does he allow any untidy twigs to protrude. The Quartets, rugged as they appear on the surface, are yet perfectly rounded and carefully wrought.

Just as in his piano music Bartók, conscious of the instrument's limitations, explores chiefly its characteristic percussive qualities, so all that he gives the string quartet to do is equally ideally adapted to the genius of each of the four solo string instruments and to the peculiar musical substance obtainable from their combination. While at the piano he is addicted to chord effects and a certain bareness, he becomes here richly polyphonic. Even though the association of the four instruments completely removes their harmonic poverty, he still treats them as essentially

* Its main outlines still survive, in the freest possible form, in the first Quartet, two of whose movements are built loosely on the symmetrical plan of A, B, A, which may be interpreted as (A) first and (B) second subject, or as (A) exposition, (B) working-out and (A) recapitulation.

melodic factors.* They wind along in great streams of melody, innumerable tributary tunes adding to the richness of the musical fabric; purely harmonic passages, although used admirably for the sake of contrast, are comparatively rare.

The first Quartet (Op. 7), written in 1908, is still to a certain extent a hybrid: a compromise between what Bartók discarded and what he strove to establish. The remnant of the sonata form, the *fugato* in the last movement, the final *stretto*, show that he is as yet only with one foot in the argosy that is to carry him to a land of new discoveries; but in the second Quartet (Op. 17), composed between 1915 and 1917, he has reached this strange territory and, by means of the intermittent works, already made himself so completely at home there that he is ready to undertake the most daring adventures.

There is nothing "pretty" about Bartók's quartets. His harmony will, for a time, prove very disconcerting to many, although it seems inconceivable how anyone could help seeing that it naturally and inevitably proceeds from the man's individuality. His physiognomy, capable of an infinity of different expressions, is often distorted into a grimace when he is strongly

* In the Violin and Piano Sonatas we find the two instruments supplementing each other most admirably, each adhering throughout to its own characteristic features.

moved to express an overpowering feeling. His music has not the well-bred indifference of mediocrity : it is passionately serious, and even in its humorsome moments never flippant. Formality of any kind a composer with so clear a sense of natural proportion can well afford to despise ; economy of material must obviously be distasteful to a man of such abundant invention, who need not be concerned with the niggardly methods of the *bourgeois* musician who keeps every thematic scrap in his stock-pot in order to serve it up on the next suitable occasion ; neither does his music know the aristocratic restraint that taboos as bad form any reference to sincere feeling. Bartók's music is comparable to peasant art in its crudeness, its natural humour and its undisguised emotion.

To appreciate the Quartets it is essential that the hearer should first detach his mind from all preconceived ideas of what chamber music ought to be. Only then will he be able to see the primitive and yet refined beauty of these works, and only then will they make the deep impression they are capable of making on an unbiassed listener. It is all a matter of point of view. A Hungarian peasant who knows nothing about "art music" would probably think Bartók a maker of great music and the classics fussy and highly artificial pedants. We are at last beginning to be a little less diffident in saying it openly if a certain work of Bach, Beethoven or Brahms bores us, and perhaps the day is not too far distant on which people will tell each other candidly when they recognize the fine qualities of so perplexing a personality as Béla Bartók.

XXIII. A MUSICAL NOVEL BY FREDERICK DELIUS

XXIII. A MUSICAL NOVEL BY FREDERICK DELIUS

"FENNIMORE and Gerda" by Frederick Delius is, wisely, not described as an opera by the composer, who simply calls the work "two Episodes from the life of Niels Lyhne, in eleven scenes, after the novel by J. P. Jacobsen."

In adapting the work of the great Danish novelist to the stage, Delius undertook a task for which, though it bristles with difficulties and pitfalls, he is singularly fitted. It is hard to imagine another composer setting, or wishing to set, such a work to music, or to think of anyone who would have done it nearly so well. It was necessary, first of all, in order to retain some of the lyrical atmosphere of Jacobsen's book, to dispense with anything that looks even remotely like operatic convention, and it is remarkable to find how Delius has dissociated his mind from every known form of opera, and how the new form adopted by him not only seems to fit the subject like a glove, but is particularly capable of conveying some of the curiously bitter-sweet flavour of the novel.

"Niels Lyhne" is written in that nervous, hypersensitive and feverishly passionate style which makes Jens Peter Jacobsen stand alone in the literature of his country, which is, indeed, not quite like anything else in the world. Mr.

Edmund Gosse has very shrewdly pointed out in his preface to the English translation, that in searching for a parallel figure in literature, one is guided to think of the names of poets, not of prose writers, that the reader enjoys the book as a poem rather than as a novel, and that what matters is not so much what is related as the manner in which it is told. Every page leaves a satisfying impression of musical cadences rarely found in narrative prose.

That such a work is not easily turned into an opera, may be readily understood, for though it has as it were a musical texture in the original, it is precisely this delicacy of style which must needs evaporate as soon as an attempt, however skilful and sympathetic, is made to turn it into stage values. Another feature of Jacobsen which must be inevitably impaired by converting his work into a libretto, is the subtlety of his psychology, that painfully, morbidly minute analysis of his characters, which pries with the cruel deliberation of the vivisector into every emotion of those sensitive creatures who are mercilessly tossed about and battered by life. But if this psychology can at least be partially transmitted to the stage, the same cannot be said of Jacobsen's marvellous lyrical gift of describing nature and conjuring up the whole environment in which the story is set, that subtle charm of the Danish countryside, under whose smiling neatness there seems to

PORTRAIT BY AXEL HELSTED, 1884.

lurk some curiously indefinite bitterness. In "Niels Lyhne" the intertwining of these melancholy pictures with the moods of the soul, so elusive that one must almost despair of describing it, is fixed here and there with extraordinary precision by a few words of studied and yet natural simplicity. Jacobsen has a great power, also, of describing interiors and giving them just the note that he requires for his background. The snow-white curtains, the polished mahogany, the portraits of these old-fashioned Danish country houses, everything is graphically, though never photographically, visualized until we seem to breathe that peculiar mixture of indefinable perfumes and odours that pervade every house. The fragrance and delicate beauty of flowers very frequently plays a principal part in creating Jacobsen's atmosphere; so passionately did he love them that they almost assumed the importance of living beings, both in his life and in his work.

Obviously enough, in the operatic version all these sutbleties become attenuated and the loss is but imperfectly compensated for by scenic devices. So far as it is possible, however, to make a dramatic work out of an essentially lyrical one, the attempt made in "Fennimore and Gerda" is undeniably successful. The action is kept as closely to the main events of the novel as possible, snatches of dialogue being transferred bodily into it and descriptive passages turned into stage directions and scenic pictures. The compromise of cutting had to be resorted to, but no disturbing alien matter has at any rate been added; it must, however, be confessed that the pruning-knife has in at least one place not been applied with sufficient skill to prevent a serious mutilation, which throws the whole work sadly out of balance and destroys the pessimistic note which is too essential a feature of the novel to justify any interference. The central idea of the book, distasteful as it may be, does not admit of the happy ending adopted for the musical version and cannot be sacrificed without incurring the danger of making the work entirely episodic. This central idea, which runs as an undercurrent through the novel from beginning to end, is based on the theory that freethinkers, however defiant their views, must under pressure of impending great calamities find, in the author's own words, "the liberty they had gained too heavy a burden for their shoulders and, obedient to the siren voices* of tradition and the memories of childhood on the one side, and the censoriousness of society on the other, bend their knees and appeal to Heaven for help." The tragic conflict arises out of these people's consciousness of having been faithless to their own convictions. The

* The English translation appeared under the title of *Siren Voices* (Heinemann).

pessimistic drift of the novel, having its root in this underlying theory, cannot be altered without undermining the whole edifice. The operatic version therefore, in spite of the fact that it ends happily with Niels' betrothal to Gerda, leaves us with a vague, uneasy feeling that all is not well, that something has been suppressed which in the interests of dramatic truth should have been told, and we cannot whole-heartedly share the joyous excitement of the bride's young sisters in the final scene, charming though it is in itself. Somewhere in the middle of the work, it would have served as a delightful contrast, but at the end it strikes a false note. It is rather like turning "Richard Feverel" into a play and ending with the marriage of Richard and Lucy, in order to send the audience home happy, and snugly ignorant of the inevitably tragic end designed by Meredith.

This being said, the libretto must be accepted as a very skilful piece of work. That it leaves a mere skeleton of Jacobsen's story is in the nature of things, and no arranger could have succeeded in transplanting all its poetical atmosphere to the stage. But now comes Frederick Delius, whose music, in some inexplicable way, actually succeeds in restoring to it that peculiar perfume of Jacobsen's luxuriant style. Everything in his work, moreover, sounds so spontaneous and natural that one cannot detect any effort on his part to catch the right note; he seems simply to have remained himself and relied upon some curious poetical affinity between his own nature and that of Jacobsen's to lead his inspiration into the right channel. The two artists have, indeed, much in common. There is the same disdainful aloofness from all that is obvious and superficially pleasing, the same attention to elaborate but always subordinate detail, the same delicate hues of light and shade, the same transmutation of everything into artistic values. It is therefore not surprising that sometimes a simple cadence or an exquisite phrase strikes us like the very echo of the novelist's thought, although it would be impossible to say why it is just this or that phrase or cadence that has such an effect. Perhaps Delius himself could not tell; his music does not sound reasoned, it sounds instinctively felt.

But the work is remarkable in another respect. It is cast in a form unlike that of any other musical stage work ever written. Delius has followed no precedent, least of all the one that is most wonderful in itself and most pernicious in its influence—that of Wagner. In spite of a few thematic references, which are no more than fleeting thoughts of the past, he has nothing to do with the *Leitmotiv*, that coldly logical deputy of inspiration. The invention of Frederick Delius flows incessantly onwards and when he has exhausted a musical idea, or rather before it is exhausted, he leaves it behind and has no need to fall back on it because fresh thoughts refuse to come. Thus, when once in a way he does refer back to a phrase heard earlier in the work, the quotation gives us the impression of a spontaneous poetical reminiscence and not that of a stop-gap. He never handles a phrase longer than it can bear. His method may be compared to that of a poet who has found a happy metaphor; he will follow it up and develop it throughout a whole stanza, but discard it as soon as he has extracted its full meaning. One cannot speak of any thematic development in "Fennimore and Gerda," for no musical idea in the work really assumes the proportions or the importance of a theme. It must be said, in fact, that we have here an opera written almost without a single tune. All those who are familiar with Delius' work know that melodic invention is not his strong point, and that at most he is happy in finding good phrases. This opera, if it contains no real melody, is certainly full of such exquisite phrases, which are spun out for a little while, then with a soft curve flow into new delicious ideas, those again giving way to another train of thoughts. Thus a shimmering, translucent tissue is woven which folds itself gently round the action without ever becoming obtrusive or blatant, making an infinitely delicate background for the pictures that unfold themselves before us. There is a curious unity about the whole work, which makes it appear as steeped in one atmosphere from beginning to end. No dramatic over-emphasis, no violent climax is allowed to intrude. The music remains reticent, even at the most dramatic moments. The composer refuses to speak loudly to attract those who remain in the distance; only those who are willing to approach him will hear his message. This reserve is not due to any want of confidence, but rather to a fastidiousness of feeling, which prefers delicate allusion to coarse and more direct methods. This aristocratic feeling so distinguishes the music to "Fennimore and Gerda" that, strangely enough, its evident lack of real dramatic power appears as a virtue instead of a blemish. Operas of a more robust type (such as "Tosca" or "Louise") would collapse at once in this rarefied atmosphere; its drowsy and alluring perfume would not let them live a moment; but for Jacobsen it is the very breath of life.

One of the greatest virtues of the work is its wonderful conciseness. There is neither a word nor a note too much. It is concerned, both dramatically and musically, with essentials. The eleven scenes into which it is divided are extremely short, sometimes only of the duration of a few words, a snatch of conversation. As an instance of the terseness of the action it may be mentioned that the part of Fennimore's mother consists of exactly fourteen words. We are given mere glimpses of just as much as we need to know, and we are consequently gripped by a sense of intense, closely moving drama. Take, for example, the growing misunderstanding between Erik and Fennimore, which is shown to us in all its tragic intensity in a few words, and compare it with the endless and tortuous argument between Wotan and Fricka (to mention one of the worst examples of disastrous verbosity in Wagner), where the situation of the henpecked god in the clutches of the nagging goddess, logically developed as it is dramatically, becomes musically so disproportionate as to strike the hearer as both tiresome and ludicrous. Delius, like Mozart and Moussorgsky, and unlike Wagner, understood the essential difference between a spoken and a musical form of dramatic art and between the distinct ways in which they reach the hearer. This is the secret why in spite of his wholly undramatic music, his work moves forward at a breathless, stirring pace.

Where many another composer would have filled twenty pages of introduction to tell us that he is going to start, Delius begins without introduction at all. A phrase of one bar, and we are in the midst of the first scene.

The dialogue, in prose, which often comes straight out of the novel, is quite simple, just the talk of ordinary people; and yet about everything even about such commonplaces as "Don't trouble, Uncle," or "Make yourself comfortable," there is a glamour of that poetry which Delius seems to have transferred from the book into his score. Jacobsen made the most lyrical novel out of an unlyrical subject; Delius makes the most deeply musical work out of an unmusical libretto.

Some short outlines of the drama and the music are best left to go hand in hand. But as already hinted, there are no outstanding musical features, and it is almost as impossible to pick out anything from the score to give an idea of the whole, as it would be to demonstrate the effect of a Turkey carpet by drawing one or two of its arabesques separately on a blackboard.

The first scene discloses the home of Fennimore's parents, where her two cousins, Niels Lyhne and Erik Refstrup, are spending a holiday. They both love Fennimore, but she has eyes only for Erik. The fine intimacy of the family gathered together while the rain is pouring down outside, may at once be cited as an instance of the poetical significance given by the refined musical illustration to what would otherwise be quite an ordinary scene. Fennimore is asked to sing, and she complies with a song that introduces a dash of local colour. It is one of those conventional ballads, with the rather insipid air and the tamely sentimental words so frequently found in Scandinavian music, of which the ordinary

Northern people are so fond. Delius' imitation is almost perfect, although even here we find that curiously wavering melodic line into which he nearly always falls when a straightforward tune is required of him. The phrase on which the curtain rises is used a good deal at first; it is one of those motives which Delius handles just as long as he pleases and then leaves aside.

The first scene is connected with the next by a lengthy orchestral interlude, preparing us for the garden scene at night on which the curtain is about to open, and which is steeped in that atmosphere Delius is so fond of and renders to such perfection, as all those know who have heard his " In a Summer Garden " or " Summer Night on the River." There is the little wistful fragment, the rocking figure that suggests a boat on the moonlit water, and the languid voice singing passionately afar off. Here occurs the love scene between Erik and Fennimore, overheard by the despairing Niels, and an entrancingly beautiful phrase is heard. The word " theme " must be avoided in a description of this music, for even though a few passages recur in the course of the work, they are still no more than singularly beautiful snatches of melody which seem to haunt us later on with a kind of tragic irony. There are no " leading motives," no tags hung on to a situation, otherwise they would have to be resorted to with pedantic logic at every turn throughout the development of the drama.

Three years elapse between the garden scene and the next, where we meet Erik and Fennimore again at their house on the edge of the sea, married and disillusioned. His ambition as a painter is gone, his inspiration lost, their love all but shattered. They have invited Niels in the hope that he might help and advise Erik, and now follows the pitiable story of how Niels and Fennimore gradually drift, from very hopelessness, into a passionate, irresistible attachment, Erik's dissolute habits in which he hopes to drown his disappointments, dealing the death-blow to his wife's loyalty. In a series of seven scenes, which run one into the other with but one interruption in the music, this tale is unfolded in its essential features. The music has become harder, as it were, and though it is always full of poetic feeling, it has no longer that luxuriant loveliness of the first two scenes. We stand before crude facts, before pitiless truth. But occasionally, especially in the interludes between the scenes, the tragedy is softened down to a note of pathos that is almost unbearable in its poignancy. There is something indefinably moving in simple passages like the one that occurs between the third and fourth scenes, where the curtain is lowered but for an instant.

The atmosphere is admirably reflected, again, in

the music to such scenes as that where Fennimore is found asleep at dawn after waiting up all night for Erik, or to the despairing, unhappy love scene between Niels and Fennimore in the autumnal forest, which is accompanied by uneasily shifting chromatic passages.

A beautiful reminiscence of the love scene in the garden between Erik and Fennimore is heard, when the latter tells Niels that she has already pondered too much over her lost love for her husband. The touch of exquisitely subtle tragedy lies in the harmonic and melodic change which the music has undergone. Fennimore no longer thinks of the incident with the same feeling; it has become tainted and tinged with vain regrets.

The dramatic climax of Erik's sudden death by an accident, and the psychological change in Fennimore, who, from that moment begins to hate Niels with a fanatical hatred, is treated in a harsh, feverish manner that is most appropriate.

Another interval of three years leads us to the episode of Gerda, but not before we have seen, as a complete contrast, the quiet picture of Niels at his old home, which is very wisely interpolated as a suggestion of rest and forgetfulness between the two love episodes, which might otherwise clash rather disagreeably. We are given a glimpse of one of those lovely harvest pictures in rural Denmark, which have a detachment from all the turmoils of life and a feeling of contentment in simple, calmly beautiful things, which are not found quite like this anywhere else in the world. The captivating pastoral introduction and the song of the farm labourers in the fields convey this atmosphere extremely well. Between this scene and the following, there is an exquisite idyllic interlude, and we now enter upon the final picture, laid in the old-fashioned garden of Gerda's father, with the lovely and yet unfortunate scene of the betrothal. Delius does not appear to be very happy with Gerda's three romping little sisters, but it is easily imagined how delicately he handles the love scene between the disillusioned man and the romantic young girl, into which he infuses a mixed feeling of hope and regret. In this mood the opera ends.

To stage the work must be an expensive venture, for, short as it is, it requires a greater number of scenic changes than most full-grown operas. And perhaps the delicacy of this music is hardly calculated to withstand the necessarily somewhat coarse conditions of a stage performance. At the piano, imperfectly as one can realize the whole effect, one has the impression that "Fennimore and Gerda" should draw the hearer irresistibly into that poetical sphere in which the work seems to live. Even the somewhat sordid theme should not prevent this, for its realistic harshness is softened in the opera by the music of Frederick Delius, as it is in the book by the poetry of Jens Peter Jacobsen.

XXIV. A LATE STRAUSS OPERA

XXIV. A LATE STRAUSS OPERA

THOSE who have watched the gradual decline of Strauss's inspiration, which begins to become distinctly traceable from act to act of "Der Rosenkavalier" and reaches through "Ariadne auf Naxos" a stage of utter degeneracy in the bombastic inanities of the "Alpine Symphony," may not unreasonably be prepared to witness a total collapse of inventive power in a later work for the stage, "Die Frau ohne Schatten." However, all save the composer's worst enemies will be, as his compatriots put it, "agreeably disappointed" to find that he has once more rallied an unexpected amount of strength. The greater part of "The Woman without a Shadow," while it is debatable whether it is good music, must at any rate be acknowledged to be very good Strauss. It is true that it contains little that is new : the impression is that of an epitome of all that is best in the earlier works, of which we are continually reminded. This music is intensely personal and could not possibly be mistaken for anything but Strauss ; and it is perhaps for this very reason that nearly every passage seems to be simply a variant—sometimes a caricature and sometimes a fascinating improvement—of things with which we have long been familiar. Don Juan and Don Quixote strut gallantly through the pages of the score, Salome and Elektra make their perverse and diseased presences felt, the Rose Cavalier pays flying visits to contribute the best tunes from Vienna ; there are glimpses of the languishing Ariadne and even Till Eulenspiegel pokes in his roguish nose more than once. But, above all, Zarathustra looms large and infests everything with his philosophy, which in a loose sort of way seems to lie at the root of the obscurely symbolic and mystical libretto, with its double cast of spirits and humanity whose actions and whose fate are closely linked together. Needless to say, all these familiar figures are dressed up in new and often very attractive musical costumes, but their faces remain those we have all known of old.

" Die Frau ohne Schatten " is the joint product of Strauss's all but indissoluble partnership with Hugo von Hofmannsthal, who has given a further proof of his alarming versatility by essaying an entirely new subject, a symbolic-philosophic fairy tale that lends itself to a great display of brilliant stagecraft and to exactly the kind of superficially intellectual musical illustration that Strauss excels in. The libretto, with its deliberately obscure and rather clumsy allegory posing as profound mysticism, is far too involved to make a successful opera, in spite of its many picturesque aspects that lend themselves well to musical treatment. It is a kind of modern and very sophisticated " Magic Flute " with all the

SCENIC DESIGN FOR "DIE FRAU OHNE SCHATTEN" BY P. ARAVANTINOS.

esoteric confusion but without the engaging *naïveté* of its prototype. The very title is symbolic. The woman, a kind of feminine Peter Schlemihl, who barters her shadow, typifies the evasion of the duty of motherhood, and it is round this problem that the whole plot turns. Both the supernatural and the human beings become involved in it in some way or another, only to triumph in the end after having been tried in the fire of tragic guilt.

Unfortunately the author has treated his subject in a strictly literary rather than in a musical manner, and he has consequently denied Strauss the opportunity of freeing himself from the thraldom of the "leading motive." As the libretto stands, it would have been impossible for the composer to set it to absolute music, even if he had wished to do so, because too much in the text depends on verbal explanation and needs to be further elucidated by the music. The underlying impelling force who directs the ordeals wherewith both the spirits and the human beings are to be tried, the Sorcerer Keikobad, never appears on the stage, and there is no other means of bringing the importance of his functions home to the audience than by a *Leitmotiv*. It must be acknowledged that Strauss uses this resource with consummate mastery. In his hands it becomes a pliable material, which he weaves into a tissue of sound that is symphonic, instead of being merely logical in a literary rather than a musical sense. But wherever the text does compel its literary use, as in the case of the Keikobad motive, it remains as rigid and lifeless as ever.

A flagrant defect of this opera is the fact that, the symphonic tissue being very closely woven and of the utmost significance, the voice parts generally lack all organic connection with it. They give the impression of having been, more often than not, grafted on to the finished polyphonic background. The voices are therefore too unimportant and drift about without blending with the rest ; they are like recitatives used to connect the great points of repose, as in the old operas they connect the arias and ensembles, only that here they far less frequently drive to such purely musical culminating points and so become considerably overweighted. The music hovers between the old and the new, and never grows into a complete organism. Wherever an ensemble occurs, the relapse into older operatic forms only serves to enhance this impression, although the characters are never allowed to stand in a row behind the footlights and to address the audience ; the action continues uninterruptedly, and it is only at points where a logical concerted passage is dramatically justified that the singing voices are combined. On the whole, one may rejoice that Strauss should have abandoned here and there the exclusive sway of the Wagnerian dialogue and soliloquy in favour of the essentially musical concerted expression.

The thematic material of the opera is extraordinarily rich and incisive. Everything is aptly characterized by very plastic motives, some of which are of ethereal beauty, others of workaday ugliness. There is music expressive of superhuman serenity and music telling of human misery ; some of the themes rise up boldly and trenchantly, others are uneasy, shifting and of sinister import ; those connected with the spirit-world are solemn and aloof, while those of the human beings, according to their varying characters, express everything from low grasping vulgarity and nagging ill-temper to simple tenderness and gentle forbearance. All these strands of thematic invention are gathered into magnificent symphonic pictures, but they share the inevitable fate of the "leading motive" which, however appropriate it may be as long as it remains connected with the character or the situation of which it is born, makes it impossible for the composer to sustain a definite mood for any length of time or to reach a climax by degrees. Instead of imparting to each scene a distinct atmosphere, Strauss, by continually drawing on all these snatches of thought, rarely contrives to build up a sustained development of any musical idea.

One instance will suffice to illustrate clearly how the *Leitmotiv* destroys all hope of attaining to unity of colour. In the opening scene the Nurse, the evil spirit of the piece, confers with a messenger from Keikobad about the latter's daughter, who is irresistibly drawn towards humanity by a mysterious sympathy. Now, the themes typifying the Nurse are malevolent, caustic, ugly things which exactly describe her character ; but as soon as she refers to Keikobad's daughter we hear in the orchestra the latter's beautiful theme, and a feeling of pure serenity prevails that is dramatically entirely unjustified, since it is still the Nurse we behold on the stage and her evil purposes we listen to. And so the kaleidoscopic accompaniment changes continually, and it depends entirely upon chance whether the leading motives referred to happen to fit in with the mood or whether they defeat their own aim of underlining and intensifying it. The true function of music in opera should be simply to heighten the emotion hidden in the text, to express all those things that the words can only hint at ; instead of this, we find here that the music merely conveys the message of the tale over again through a second medium, so that we have the whole story told us at one and the same time, word for word as it were, in two different languages. Each of these two complete things, the fully developed drama and the organic symphonic poem, would be better without the other. There is no doubt that the " leading motive " is the ideal medium for the symphonic poem, where it is left to describe audibly some dramatic incident that would otherwise remain incomprehensible, but it is emphatically the wrong medium for opera.

If "Die Frau ohne Schatten" is bad opera, this is mainly the fault of the poet, for it is certainly a wonderful, glowing symphonic poem. One may dislike Strauss, with his gaudiness, his vacillating style, his rapid descents from sublimity to vulgarity, his aggressively dazzling orchestration that never yields a moment's repose, his unrestrained dramatic over-emphasis ; but it is impossible to deny that this work almost consistently represents him at his best. There are pages of great beauty, especially in the music between the scenes, a fact that supports the argument that as soon as we shut out the stage, the *Leitmotiv* becomes a valuable asset. The transformation music between the first two scenes, descriptive of the flight to earth from the regions of the spirit-world, is very fine : the lofty thematic material gradually seems to become tainted with everyday sordidness, until the curtain opens upon the squalor of the poor dyer's dwelling, with the ignoble brawl of his brothers.

This contrast between beauty and ugliness once again throws into relief a feature that has ever been characteristic of Strauss's music. He is still unable to convey the former by anything but the diatonic system, and for the latter he invariably resorts to chromatic distortions of it. He is chained as fast as ever to the orthodox major and minor scales, and still rejects any of the numerous innovations that have sprung up since the days of his youth. Strauss is not really a " modern " composer, for no amount of chromatic divagation can hide his allegiance to the diatonic scales. The latter represent for him musical beauty, a state of health ; whatever is deliberately discordant in his music is for him a disease, a necessary evil for the sake of contrast, the vice that only exists in order that virtue may appear the more glorious. The apotheosis with which " Die Frau ohne Schatten " ends is set to pages of unadulterated C major, which unfortunately to some of us who have learnt that beauty can dwell in other modes and keys, or even in no key at all, makes this peroration fall hopelessly flat. If perfect bliss were only to be attained by a renunciation of all sharps and flats, it is to be feared that we should very soon grow weary of it.

XXV. THE CAROL REVIVED

XXV. THE CAROL REVIVED

IT is a curious fact that the most ardent champions of nationalism among British musicians have left it to Arnold Bax, who never professed any such tendencies, and never consciously displayed them, to resuscitate that most characteristic manifestation of English folk-music—the Carol. It is by no means an easy task to preserve in the concert room the spirit of a type of popular song that depends so much upon a more natural environment for its effect, nor could any but a very sensitive artist have a chance of success in modernizing a form so essentially archaic in its mixture of devotion and conviviality. This, however, Arnold Bax has done with the sure touch of a mature genius in his choral settings of two Christmas songs of the fifteenth century, of the well-known song of the same period, "The Boar's Head," and of an old religious poem discovered at Balliol College, Oxford.* They are not his first experiment in this direction, for there is an earlier setting of a fifteenth-century carol, "There is no Rose of such Virtue,"† for one voice, with piano or orchestral accompaniment, composed at Christmas, 1909: a delightful song that already shows an intimate understanding of the peculiar, semi-secular and at the same time fervently devout spirit that pervades the traditional carol; but it is obvious

* Murdoch, Murdoch & Co.
† J. & W. Chester, Ltd.

that only on resorting to a choral treatment of similar texts the composer could hope to do full justice to these characteristic features. In this early setting the essentials of the carol as distinct from the anthem and hymn are not as sharply drawn as they are in three of the works to be dealt with here—" Now is the time of Christymas," " Of a Rose I sing," and " The Boar's Head."

The most successful is, perhaps, the first, the music of which reflects to perfection the boisterous sturdiness of words such as these :

Make me merry both more and less,
For now is the time of Christymas !

It is set for male voices, and the accompaniment is restricted to a flute and a piano. The former plays a phrase of its own, as if soliloquizing apart from the crowd, its part being written throughout in the key of C, while the others are in G. The modal impression resulting from the flattened seventh lends the piece an archaic colour that is perfectly in keeping with its mediæval spirit of riotous joy in the good things brought by Yuletide. The chorus, after exhorting all present to sing, or bring some other sport, " that it may please at this feasting," assumes a tone of half-malignant, half-frolicsome ferocity, as it lustily suggests the stocks as meet punishment for him who " can naught do."

The treatment of the voice parts, though simple in comparison with another work to be discussed presently, shows complete mastery of counterpoint. Each verse deals freely with the tune, now in vigorous unison, now fugally, and again in free part-writing, but always in a manner most appropriate to the words. The flute spins out its own theme gracefully the while, and the piano supplies characteristic touches illuminating the text.

"Of a Rose I sing" inclines to be more purely spiritual, but the distinctive quality of the carol is nevertheless unmistakable, for the words refer not only to the subject with which they deal, but to those who are engaged in the performance. Such a thought as this:

> Now Christ save all this company,
> And send us good life and long,

could not occur in any purely religious work destined for the church; it points to a folk-song, religious in character, but designed for a temporal occasion.

This Carol is written for a small choir of mixed voices, accompanied by harp, violoncello and double bass. Once more the instrumental background works out a good deal of material that is independent of the rest. It forms, so to speak, a worldly setting for the pious narrative related by the choir. Again there is no suggestion of church ; rather do we imagine a small village choir, supported by three strolling instrumentalists, performing outside a manor-house late on Christmas Eve, their lanterns throwing beams of orange-coloured light across the blue shadows of the snow, and their voices uplifted quite as much in expectation of good cheer as in religious fervour. The polyphonic writing is more elaborate than in the preceding example. In some passages the music becomes frankly descriptive, as in the setting of the words, " The fourth branch sprang into hell," where the basses give out a snarling laugh and the sopranos a doleful wail. The impression—purely as impression—is baffling and immensely effectively, but it must be confessed that it is too realistic to escape altogether the charge of being a solecism in style. The wonderful eight-part " Amen " at the end, too, is almost too cunningly contrived not to detract somewhat from the homely simplicity of a true carol.

" The Boar's Head " has no such lapses of style ; it is a pure carol, set for unaccompanied male choir or solo quartet. The religious note in it is strongly tainted with very worldly preocccupations : the joys of the table are frankly extolled in a mixture of primitive English and elementary Latin, and the Almighty receives homage merely in consideration of His being a munificent maker and donor of the good things of the earth. In Bax's music the jovial tune that illustrates the secular portions predominates accordingly; the manner in which it bursts impatiently into the Amen of the serious introduction is a subtle stroke of musical suggestion. The counterpoint is elaborate, but never pedantic, and the separate parts have a natural flow that is never checked by the intricacy with which they are intertwined.

Arnold Bax's fourth work in this form is not a carol in the accepted sense. It is true that there are three similar pieces of William Byrd extant, which are described as carols, but since the term is no longer current in connection with pure church music, the setting by Arnold Bax of "Mater ora filium" might be more properly called a motet. Written for an unaccompanied double chorus, it is purely devotional and without the admixture of profane notions that characterizes the carol as we know it to-day. The words have all the artless innocence of popular feeling, but the composer's setting lifts them on to the plane of a great piece of church music. The whole is an astounding polyphonic structure. The Latin motto with which it opens is at the same time made the leading motive musically, woven into the texture with amazing ingenuity. When this fabric has grown extraordinarily complex, a new motive on the word "Alleluia," introduced in a *fugato*, is still superadded. The work is not strictly fugal in treatment, that is to say, the different phrases in the text are not inseparably associated with definite musical subjects introduced in an academically contrapuntal manner.

Bax's polyphonic writing, in its perfect freedom, is much more akin to that of Palestrina or Byrd than to that of Bach and Handel. But it always remains polyphonic with admirable consistency; the whole choral structure is made up of the horizontal filaments of strict part-writing, and even where occasional passages occur that look like shifting blocks of chords rather than separately moving voices, they appear to be the result of a clashing of the parts deliberately calculated to produce such a result, and not a relapse into vertical chord progressions. Bax very rightly sees no reason why he should not use such modern sound-values when he feels that they supply his needs. He is, after all, a composer of to-day, and although he sets out here to recapture the spirit of the old polyphonic masters, he does not aim at a slavish imitation of the contrapuntal music of the past. It is the more astonishing to see how he has succeeded in adapting its immortal beauty to a choral music that speaks to us in the language of our own time.

To deck out archaic forms in a modern garb is not without its dangers, however, for it is but too easy for a composer to be under the impression that he is doing something really novel when he is perhaps only twisting old formulas into new shapes. This danger, which Bax has skirted once or twice in "Mater ora filium," grew into a serious menace in another sacred work of his, the unaccompanied Motet, "This Worldes Joie," the excessive chromaticism of which is liable to trick the hearer into undue astonishment at a complexity that is more apparent than real, and induces him to take for a new idiom what has its basis in very venerable procedures.

The work gives the impression that the composer was attracted by the literary, not by the spiritual quality of the words, and the result is a certain lack of conviction and truly musical emotion, in spite of its immense intellectual appeal. Although this Motet does not properly belong to the subject of the present study, its comparison with the Carols is of the greatest interest, for it shows how much more of a stylist a composer remains when he deals with a species of art that lays no constraint upon his temperament. In music that expresses purely religious emotions, Arnold Bax is not wholly at his ease, because in this particular case he has need of a literary stimulus that is merely secondary to the subject he sets out to treat; but the Carol, which has hitherto been wholly neglected as a serious form of art by composers of note, made an immediate and definitely musical appeal to him, and thus found in him an admirable and most welcome restorer.

INDEX

INDEX

INDEX

INDEX

INDEX

INDEX

INDEX

INDEX

INDEX

INDEX

INDEX

INDEX

INDEX

INDEX

INDEX

INDEX

INDEX

INDEX